redeeming
POWER

"This book gave me fresh, practical, and atypically positive insights into my own use of power in leadership. Ann Garrido has helped me reflect on the leadership actions I take every day as creative opportunities to participate in building God's Kingdom."

Crystal Caruana Sullivan
Executive Director of Campus Ministry, University of Dayton

"Profound, impactful, moving. In a simple and brilliant way, Ann Garrido prompts us to become the leaders God called us to be. Her storytelling grants you the opportunity to experience Christ and to delight daily in his power. As a Catholic educator, I find this work is a beautiful, necessary reminder for me not only of who I am, but whose I am."

Ashley Rae Mathis
Head of School, Notre Dame High School, San Jose, California

"Ann Garrido's analysis of power for contemporary Catholic leaders will open your eyes to various dimensions of this human capacity, which Christians too often refer to pejoratively. We all must use and experience power, and Garrido's exploration of it within the Christian context will help leaders be more mindful of relationships and how to use power more fruitfully."

Scott Bader
Director of Parish Financial Services, Archdiocese of Seattle

"Pastoral ministers and all Catholics who lead will find in *Redeeming Power* a book full of wonderful insights! Using Genesis and the gospels as her foundation, Ann Garrido offers twelve thought-provoking and inspiring theological reflections on the gift of power along with practical lessons and guidance from Church leaders past and present."

Brian B. Reynolds
Chancellor and Chief Administrative Officer, Archdiocese of Louisville

redeeming POWER

Exercising the Gift as God Intended
12 Lessons for Catholics Who Lead

Ann M. Garrido

AVE MARIA PRESS AVE Notre Dame, Indiana

Nihil Obstat: Reverend Monsignor Michael Heintz, PhD
Censor Librorum

Imprimatur: Most Reverend Kevin C. Rhoades
Bishop of Fort Wayne–South Bend
Given at Fort Wayne, Indiana, on 31 October, 2023

Founded in 1865, Ave Maria Press is a ministry of the United States Province of Holy Cross.

www.avemariapress.com

Paperback: ISBN-13 978-1-64680-272-2

E-book: ISBN-13 978-1-64680-273-9

Cover image © GettyImages.com.

Cover design by Samantha Watson.

Text design by Kristen Hornyak Bonelli.

Printed and bound in the United States of America.

Library of Congress Cataloging-in-Publication Data is available.

To Miguet,

who never doubts his power.

Repeat after me: I can change things. I can make something happen.

—Sr. Thea Bowman

Contents

Introduction

Two thousand years ago today—give or take a decade—a construction worker from a village of around ninety people on the edge of a vast and violent empire quit his day job. After he laid down his tool belt, no one heard from him for well over a month. But upon his return, he stood in front of a smattering of family and friends, opened the Bible (okay, unrolled—things were a little different back then), and announced that the business of the world was about to undergo a major reorganization.

Those who understood themselves to be the managers of the business of the world were not amused. Who'd died and put him in charge? Even his family and friends wondered where he got such gumption. Was he unaware that no one important came from Nazareth? But then they stood back and watched as he began to not only call disciples but also call the shots. They watched as he started to issue judgments, cross boundaries, and set new ones. Let's be clear: he was a nobody—a carpenter, not a king; a Jew, not a Roman. Yet he walked around generously giving away what was his as if he were a millionaire, not a pauper. He was confrontational, was unconcerned about the opinions of others, and treated the rules as if they did

1

not apply to him—all classic behaviors of persons with power. So, just who did he think he was?

It is probably a question you've also been asked at some point: "Just who do you think you are?" Because you, too, are a person of power. You, too, have followers. True, they probably haven't sold their boats and dedicated their lives to you, but they do listen to what you say and watch what you post. In their world, you, too, call the shots. Not *all* the shots, you might protest. Okay. But the decisions you make affect their lives. They report to you or sit in your classroom or fill the pews of your church. When you are in contact with the power you have, you, too, are likely perceived by them as outspoken and recklessly free, maybe even a little (or maybe a lot) threatening. "Just who do you think you are?" is a question commonly asked of those coming into their power. Those who already hold power ask it to you aloud. Those who don't, just think it in their minds.

But how do you feel when you hear me call you a "person of power"? Proud? Awkward? Confused? I think I can see you squirm a bit even from here. Is that who *you* think you are? For some of us in Christian leadership, it is a label with which we can readily identify. For many of us, though, being called a person of power is uncomfortable: Are you saying I'm corrupt? Intimidating? Abusive? Perhaps a "person of influence" might work, but in this era of social media influencers, even that designation feels dicey. Do you think I'm manipulative? A sellout? Maybe a "person of authority" would be better. But then it sounds like I'm dictatorial. High and mighty. And, besides, there are all these things I *can't* do. Things I *can't* make happen. Don't you see that?

I do. I share many of your hesitancies about being labeled a person of power. In the writing of this book, I interviewed around forty Christian leaders who hold a wide variety of formal and informal roles in church, business, and non-profit organizations. And they all said much the same. These were bishops and CEOs, popular preachers and school administrators, pastors and vice-presidents in health care. They were teachers and well-known bloggers, founders of new movements and entrepreneurs. They all expressed a degree of uneasiness. It's hard to know what to do with a label like "person of power."

What makes it hard is that all of us have stories in our minds about what being a person of power means, and many of them are not good. Pick up any book on the subject of power right now—be it in the philosophy, politics, business, or leadership theory section of the bookstore—and it will very likely begin with an abbreviated version of Lord Acton's famous quote: "Power corrupts, and absolute power corrupts absolutely."[1] If you turn the pages seeking a definition of power, you will most likely find the one offered by Max Weber, an early 20th century German sociologist, describing power as "the possibility within a social relationship of realizing one's own will even against resistance."[2] Continue to randomly open more volumes and you are apt to see a quote from Weber's American counterpart, C. Wright Mills: "All politics is a struggle for power; the ultimate kind of power is violence,"[3] or the 16th century political theorist Machiavelli, "He who is the cause of another becoming powerful is ruined."[4] I'm going to take a shot in the dark and guess that none of us reading this book is keen on being perceived as corrupt, forceful, violent, or self-serving. If that is what is implied by being a person of power, then count me out.

The temptation when we have such a negative story about power in our minds is to then deny that we have it. We point toward those who have more power than us and say, "Talk to them. The buck stops over there." The temptation is to blend in and say, "I'm just an ordinary person. I can't change things." But that isn't much of a solution, is it? Because without persons of power, nothing *will* change, and the world cries out for change. What the world needs isn't people who don't have power but people who use their power as Jesus used his power to make the world a more just, loving, joyous, and hospitable place—a place he called the kingdom or reign of God.

The answer is not to deny our power or abdicate it but to reground our understanding of power in a story other than that offered by Max Weber and Machiavelli. We need to reground it in the story that grounded

Jesus's understanding of power—the scriptures of his Jewish people—and, in particular, the opening pages of this story: Genesis, chapters 1–3.

Why Genesis 1–3?

Every culture on the planet has a creation story, and not because every culture has scientifically sought out how our planet came to be. That quest is a more recent phenomenon in human history. But long before there were astronomers and physicists and biologists, the elders of every culture used stories, and specifically origin stories, as a means to pass on to the next generation their deepest intuitions about life's most important mysteries—mysteries like the nature of life and death, God, what it means to be human, sex, evil, and, yes, power.

The area of the world sometimes known as the "Near East" (modern-day Iraq, Syria, Lebanon, Jordan, Israel, and Kuwait) is home to some of the oldest creation stories known to humankind. These include from ancient Babylon the *Epic of Gilgamesh* and the *Enuma Elis*, and from ancient Assyria the *Atrahasis*. These stories were part of the air that the people of this region breathed, much as stories of Adam and Eve would still be part of ours now. In fact, our stories of Adam and Eve seem to have their roots in these even older myths.

During the time in which our Jewish ancestors in faith were exiled to Babylon (around six centuries before Jesus), they would have become especially well acquainted with their Babylonian neighbors' creation stories, and when they returned from exile and began to write down their own stories for the first time, attuned listeners would have been able to hear echoes of the place where they had been.[5] These listeners would have recognized common themes of chaotic waters inhabited by sea monsters and humans fashioned out of the clay of the earth. They would be familiar with trees that promise immortality and sneaky serpents. But they also would have heard something distinct, because the insights that the Jewish elders wanted to pass on to their children—about the nature of life and death, God, what it means to be human, sex, evil, and, yes, power—were different from what their neighbors chose to pass on. These insights had been gleaned over a long time of living in a covenant relationship with the one, true God since the time of Abraham. Often the Jewish perception of the world was far more positive than that of their neighbors, and the message that the Jewish elders wanted to share was far more empowering.

A short recap for those of us who haven't been reading Genesis at Sunday school of late: In Genesis, there are actually two creation stories. In compiling the Bible, if our ancestors in faith had two stories that they felt both revealed important truths, they had no compulsion to eliminate one in order to have a single "correct" story. Rather, they would merge them or, in the case of the creation stories, keep both side by side.

The first story of creation—Genesis 1:1–2:4a—likely played a special role in Jewish temple worship. In this story, God speaks each element of creation into being in a poetic, rhythmic fashion. In the first three days, God separates light from darkness, the waters below from the sky above, and the seas from the dry land—all in order to prepare the environment. In the next three days, God fills each of these spaces—with the sun, moon, and stars; with fish and birds; and with cattle and creeping things—and then finally with humans who arrive on the scene like guests at a banquet to discover that not only everything they need but also everything they could possibly want has been prepared before their arrival. The humans are commanded to rule over all the other creatures. God names all of creation good, but at the end of the sixth day, after humans are created, God names his work *very* good. On the seventh day, God rests from the work of creation, setting aside the seventh day forevermore as "holy," thereby stitching the Jewish practice of the Sabbath into the fabric of creation. Listening to this story, one can almost picture a temple procession and hear the chanting of those gathered for worship, verse by verse celebrating the mighty works of God.

The second story of creation—found in Genesis 2:4b–3:24—is likely the older of the two stories. This story tells of a God who is at work in the mud, fashions the human (*adam*)[6] from the ground (*adamah*), and blows into the creature's nostrils God's very own breath, waking the human to life. But then the human needs a place to live, so God fashions an idyllic garden and places the human there "to till and to keep." When the human is lonely, God fills the land with creatures. But this does not meet the human's need, so in the midst of a deep sleep, a rib is removed, and upon his waking, we meet Adam and the woman who will later be named Eve.

It is this second story of creation that continues onward to describe how the woman falls prey to a shrewd serpent and eats of the forbidden Tree of Knowledge of Good and Evil before passing its fruit also to the man. This act unleashes a series of dreadful consequences that result in the man and woman being propelled from the garden, where they had previously basked in a childlike innocence, into a life filled with adult toil and suffering.

But what could these ancient tales possibly be trying to tell us about power? And why do I say they are more empowering than other creation stories of the time?

Genesis 1–3 as an Alternative Story about Power

Interestingly, many of the creation stories of the ancient Near East would be very much at home on the bookshelves housing Lord Acton, Weber, Mills, and Machiavelli. They share the perspective of human history as a constant struggle among competing interests with no overarching trajectory toward the good and no end in sight. In the Babylonian myth of the *Enuma Elis*, for example, the heavens and earth come into being through the violent slaying and dividing of a sea monster named Tiamat. Born of this great battle, the heavens and earth themselves are locked forevermore in a state of conflict. Humans in this tale are formed from the clay of the earth and the blood of Tiamat—violence running through their veins from the very beginning. They are created specifically as slaves, to prepare food for the gods. The gods have power, not humans. Indeed, much happens *to* humans in the form of fate or bad luck that they have no control over.[7]

By way of contrast, I want to lift up six points from the Genesis creation stories that prepare us to think about power in a different way.[8]

1. In Genesis, everything that is and moves and breathes on the earth or in the heavens has one source: God. There are no other deities out there. Every blade of grass, every star, every cat, every person—and that includes every king, every nurse, every maintenance worker, every pop star, every kindergarten teacher, every auto mechanic, and every military general—can all trace their origin back to the same God and will eventually be accountable to that God for how they've lived their lives.

2.   This one God is so powerful as to be able to speak
     the entire universe into being with only the words
     "Let there be." The God of Genesis struggles with
     no one, nothing. There is no battle, no violence—
     in part because, for this God, there is no scarcity.
     God's power is abundant, never runs out, and can't
     be threatened. There is always more where that
     came from. God's power overflows into not just a
     smidgeon of life but life that is itself abundant, life
     that teems and swarms and multiplies.

3.   This one, all-powerful God has chosen humans
     from among all the earth's creatures to serve as
     God's image in the world. Humans were not
     created to be slaves providing *the gods* with food.
     No, God provides *them* with food and invites—but
     never forces—them to live as God's representatives
     within creation. And the mighty powers that God
     exercises in the creation of the world—naming,
     ordering, convening, judging, and so forth—are
     powers that have now been entrusted to humans
     to exercise as well in their royal role.

4.   According to Genesis, it is not just one person—
     for example, a king—that God has chosen to be
     God's representative on earth but every human
     person. Every person has been made in God's
     image, enlivened by the breath of God. The Jewish
     elders took this belief so seriously that they did

not think it proper to image God in a statue or drawing. Rather, every person is a unique, genuine work of art, made in the likeness of God. It is not in the divine plan for some to have power and others not. *Every* person shares in God's power to name, order, convene, judge, and so forth.

5.   Sharing in God's power through the gift of rulership—what is often translated as "dominion"—is not a license to do with the earth whatever one pleases. While dominion may ring in the ear with echoes of domination or domineering, the original Latin root for the term is *domus* or "household." Humans are to exercise dominion the way that God exercises dominion, which is about tending to the common home with the love of a parent.

6.   In Genesis, the arrival of humans on the scene of creation is not the end of the story. Their arrival on the sixth day of creation points toward a seventh day of rest, harmony, and wholeness. The human exercise of power is meant to help move history in the direction of that seventh day. If history is not moving in that direction, if things go wrong with the storyline, it is not due to fate or bad luck but because humans are not exercising their God-given dominion righteously.

Why do these six points from the Genesis accounts of our beginnings matter? Because the stories that we grow up breathing in like air become the stories that we live out in our lives.

- If I believe all power comes from God and has been freely shared with me, I am not embarrassed by the topic of power and am able to think about it in positive ways, not only negative.

- If I believe power is abundant, I'm not afraid of my own power running out, and I am more disposed to share it generously. I don't enter relationships with a sense of competition.

- If I believe I'm God's representative on earth, I know that I have not only dignity but also some degree of agency, whether or not I always feel it.

- If I believe my power has a purpose—to serve history's coming seventh day—I will use my power only in ways that help bring about peace and wholeness for all of creation.

- If I believe there will come a day when I will be held accountable by God for the way I've used the power shared with me, I will develop the habit of reflecting on my use of power regularly.

I would argue that Jesus lived his power the way he did because his understanding of power was deeply rooted in the wisdom of his Jewish ancestors, expressed in a subtle yet profound way in the Genesis stories of creation. As one who exercises leadership in Jesus's name, you are invited to root your own understanding of power in these stories and both their Jewish and Christian interpretations as well. This book intends to help. Each of the twelve chapters reflects on one of the powers God exercises in the creation stories and has gifted *us* with as representatives fashioned in the divine image. For each of the powers highlighted, we'll have the opportunity as Christian leaders to consider, "What does the holy and healthy exercise of dominion look like in this arena?"

Why the Focus on Christian Leaders? Power as Both *Potentia* and *Potestas*

If every person is God's representative on earth and shares in God's power, then why issue the invitation to Christian leaders in particular? If everyone has power, shouldn't everyone read this book? Well, yes, that would make my publisher very happy, and trust me, I am all in favor. There is a reason, however, that I am focusing especially on those in leadership roles. It has to do with the fact that there is a particular kind of power we exercise as leaders.

In Latin, there are actually two words for power that, in English, we merge into one. It is one of the reasons our attempts to discuss power are often so tangled and frustrating. We are often talking about more than one thing at the same time.

The first way we use the word *power* is linked with the Latin *potentia* from which we get the words *potential* and *potency*. In this case, *power* means "the ability to do something," "the ability to make something happen," or "the capacity to affect a change." We don't necessarily do all the things we could do as humans, but we have the power or the potential to do so. In many ways, this first definition is the kind of power the earliest chapters of Genesis are primarily concerned with, at least as I've described them so far: God giving humans the ability to do the same kinds of activities that God does in creating the world. In the literature on power, this understanding of power is often referred to as "power to." It describes how humans relate to the world in general, acknowledging there is much we can do as humans that other creatures cannot.

The second way we use the word *power*, however, is linked with the Latin *potestas*. In Roman antiquity, *potestas* referred to the relationship of the paterfamilias to the rest of his household, or *domus* (hence the connection to dominion). Current literature often refers to this kind of power as "power over." Sometimes it is hard to see a relationship between the two usages of the term,[9] but perhaps we could start with the observation that while humans in general have the power to make many things happen, the actions of some have more impact than the actions of others. For example, I could tackle a robber, but the impact of my tackle is likely to be less than that of my husband who has six inches and a good number of pounds on me. We could say we both have the power to tackle, but his power in this arena is greater than mine. There exists between us a power differential.

This second way of describing power comes closer to Weber's definition: power is the probability of realizing one's own will in relation to another's. I don't think it necessarily put us in competition with one another as Weber's addition of the phrase "even against resistance" seems to imply, but it does acknowledge that power is relative. We are exercising power not just in a general way in relation to the world at large but alongside many others who have also been given the vocation of dominion.

Much discussion in recent years has focused on what makes it possible for some persons' "powers to" to have more or less impact than others. The potential sources of "power over" that have been identified are numerous, including:

- *Physical strength*: Some of us, because of physical size and strength, quite literally have more might to move things than others. Physical strength can be further enhanced by tools, including weaponry.

- *Knowledge, expertise, education, and competence*: Some of us have more information or wisdom from experience that we can use to make things happen than others.

- *Role and authority*: Some of us function within communities or institutions that have formally appointed us to undertake certain actions, including decision-making, on their behalf.

- *Economic wealth*: Some of us can purchase our way to change more readily than others.

- *Access to networks*: Some of us are connected to far more people who also have a greater ability to make things happen.

- *Charisma, attractiveness, and attitude*: Some of us, by the magnetism of our personality, sense of humor, wittiness, or good looks have more sway than others.

- *Privilege*: Some of us, through no merit or fault of our own, but because of our given race, gender, geographic location, age, or the socioeconomic class we were born into, have an easier time asserting our will than others.

- *Authenticity and integrity*: Some of us, because of our moral rectitude, especially in the areas of fidelity and honesty (or at least appearance thereof), carry more sway than others.

Some of these "powers over" are exercised more directly than others. Physical strength, for example, makes the probability of change happen through force or coercion (i.e., threat of force), whereas charisma or authenticity makes the probability of change happen through the influence of one's words or example. None of these sources of "power over" is necessarily evil.

Few of us would deny the FBI sharpshooter a gun in a desperate hostage standoff. In fact, all of these sources can be used in wicked ways as well as to wicked ends. Yet, some of these sources of "power over" are certainly more connatural with the purpose of power found in the Genesis story—peace and wholeness—than others are.

Few of us likely will enjoy *all* of these "powers over" in our lifetime, yet all of us reading this book are currently enjoying at least some of them or we wouldn't meet the description of a leader. What *is* leadership other than the capacity to impact change more than others within a certain arena? If my country is an "economic leader," it means it has a stronger economy than others. If I am an "educational leader," it means I am assumed to have more knowledge than others. If I am a "charismatic leader," it means I have more charisma than others. If there wasn't a "more-than-others" dynamic in the relationship, I wouldn't bear the label of leader. A leader is, de facto, a "person of power over," whether we are comfortable with that definition or not.

Being described as a "person of power over" can sound scary. I had just warmed you to the idea of being a person of power, and now, in adding the word *over*, I'm probably making you nervous again. This need not be the case. Both "power to" and "power over" used rightly point in the same direction—building up of the reign of God. But possessing some degree of *potestas* ("power over") in concert with one's *potentia* ("power to") does pose additional considerations for the healthy and holy living of one's dominion. As a leader, it will not be enough to reflect only on your personal gift of power. You will also need to pay special attention to the way you want to exercise your gift of power in relationship to *others* exercising *their* gift of power.

Is the righteous use of power more complicated for a leader than for other people? Yes, it is. And that is why Christian leaders need their own book on power written specifically with them in mind. If my own experience over the past several years as a conflict educator and dialogue facilitator has taught me anything, it is that questions related to power as "power over" are among the most ethically troubling, emotionally exhausting questions any person ever has to face, and a leader has to face them all the time. Having sat in on more painful conversations regarding "power over" than I can count at this point, I admit to having fewer answers now than I did ten years ago.

But one of the things I have observed is that many of us are going into these hard conversations without drawing on our Judeo-Christian tradition as a potential resource, even when these conversations are going on inside of our own faith-based institutions. That has felt to me to be a gap. We are heirs to a remarkable inheritance—a wisdom that has been nurtured and built upon for four millennia. When we neglect spiritual tradition as one of our greatest and most valuable sources of insight and strength in tough times, our conversations and our relationships are poorer for it. I don't have definitive answers to the seemingly impossible dilemmas we are wrestling with as leaders right now, but in this book I want to offer a scripturally grounded framework in which to consider them.

If Jesus's life offers any clues, it is safe to assume Christian leadership is never going to be an easy task. It will always involve struggles and temptations and tough queries concerning the righteous use of power. There will always be folks looking at us and wondering both aloud and in the silence of their hearts, "Just who do they think they are?" But while the question is always going to be uncomfortable, it remains an important one for each of us to ponder. Who we think we are shapes everything we do. If we get the answer to that question wrong, there is very little with power that we are going to be able to get right. So let's delve into Genesis and the rich history of Jewish and Christian interpretation surrounding the creation stories to see if we might steep ourselves in the wisdom of these texts as Jesus did and become the leaders God has made us from the dawn of time to be.

1. Exercising the Power to Work with Our Hands

> The Lord God formed the man out of the dust of the ground and blew into his nostrils the breath of life, and the man became a living being. The Lord God planted a garden in Eden, in the east, and placed there the man whom he had formed. . . . The Lord God then took the man and placed him in the garden of Eden, to cultivate and care for it.
>
> —Genesis 2:7–8, 15

In Hebrew, the book of Genesis is called *B'reisheit* because *b'reisheit* is the first word of the text: "In the beginning." But do you want to know the second word in all of scripture? It is the verb *bara'* or "create." The first act of power ever associated with God is the act of creating.

Bara' is a word that is only ever associated with God. No one else in the Bible creates. And for God it seems to come so easily: "Let there be," says the first story of creation repeatedly. It is such an interesting phrase—so different from "Make it so."[1] God's first act of power involves a sort of contracting, making space for "otherness" to exist. And as the verses proceed, the phrase continues to evolve. "Let the earth bring forth vegetation." "Let the waters bring forth swarms of living creatures." "Let the earth bring forth . . . tame animals, crawling things, and every kind of wild animal." "Let there be" allows things to come into being in their own organic way like a line drawing that others get to shade with color or a hummed melody awaiting orchestration. But something shifts dramatically in Genesis 1:26 when the phrase changes to "Let us make." God is about to get personally involved in the creation of the human.

The hands-on involvement of God in the arrival of the human is even more explicit in Genesis 2. The second story of creation opens with a picture of God kneeling in the dirt and forming (*va-yitzer*) the human as a potter (*yotzer*) twisting and molding clay with his hands. Or as the eleventh-century Jewish scholar Rashi highlights, God acts like a baker who adds water to his dough and kneads it. Rashi notes, "Everything else was created by an act of speech; only man was created with the hands of God, as it is said, 'You placed your hands upon me' (Psalms 139:5)."[2]

Technically speaking, humans do not create—*bara'*—anything. And yet, the ability to take the stuff of earth up into our hands and work with it to become something new—something it could never have become on its own—is the first power that God shares with us. One could argue that animals, too, shape the earth through their daily activities, and some even use basic tools to change their environment. But for better or worse, no creature can use their hands as we can use ours—continuing to mold clay and bake bread, but also to hew timber, build cathedrals, till soil, and paint frescos. The revolutionary educator Maria Montessori (whom we will meet at the end of this chapter) once quipped that *Homo sapiens* ("the wise ones") was a misnomer; better would be *Homo laborans*, "the ones who work."

As adults, we sometimes talk of work as mere toil and drudgery, a punishment for sin assigned to us after the Fall. But note that even before the serpent ever appears on the scene, God has already placed the human (*adam*) in the garden "to till and to tend it." We who have been created by God's hand are given the gift to work with our hands, continuing the work of creation. Structures of sin can warp the way we work, forcing us to work long hours with little reward or to engage in repetitive actions as cogs in a machine rather than being able to enjoy seeing a project through from beginning to end. Sin can diminish the joy of work. It can make it difficult to find work at a salary sufficient to provide for a family. But the ability to work in itself is fundamental to the human vocation in the world.

Montessori noted this core vocation of the human is most evident in children who, from the earliest days of life, seek to encounter the world through their hands and then, as soon as they can crawl and walk, show a profound desire to involve themselves in the tasks of daily life that we as adults consider a nuisance—folding laundry, sweeping the floor, and washing dishes. Whereas it is common to hear adults refer to young children's activity as "play," Montessori observed the care and solemnity with which children undertake these tasks when allowed to do so. She also took note of the joy small children experience when they see a task through to completion. "The child is a worker and a producer," she noted. "He has his own, a great, important, difficult work indeed— the work of producing man. . . . The child's work is done unconsciously, in abandonment to a mysterious spiritual energy. . . . It is indeed a creative work; it is perhaps the very spectacle of the creation of man, as symbolically outlined in the Bible."[3]

Those working in the field of cognitive science are only now discovering how important work of the hand is in developing human intellect. We have long known that, evolutionarily, the ability to communicate via gesture preceded the ability to communicate by speech and that even today, infants are able to gesture months before they can talk. It's now becoming clear that not only is gesturing with the hand an essential step in the process of acquiring new vocabulary and grammar as a child[4] but also adults often gesture with their hands as part of working through new concepts.[5] Perhaps this is why the language we use to describe new learning is often "hand" language: "I *grasp* what you are saying." "I compre*hend*." "Do you appre*hend*?"[6] It is through the hand we continue to process our experience in this world and grow from it.

Throughout scripture, the work of the hand is understood as important preparation for leadership. Repeatedly the Bible makes specific note of what people were doing before they were called by God, as if there were a link between that work and their new role. Both Moses and David were shepherds of flocks before they were entrusted with the shepherding of the people of Israel. Amos was a "dresser of sycamores" before being called to take a verbal axe to the shrine at Bethel as a prophet. Elisha plowed with twelve yokes of oxen before uprooting everyone's expectations as a miracle worker.

And, of course, Jesus was a *tekton*—which could be translated as either "carpenter" or "stonemason"— before becoming "the stone that the builders rejected" who has "become [our] cornerstone" (Mt 21:42). He called fishermen to catch people instead. And his parables are rife with examples of the reign of God imaged as humans working with their hands: the woman kneading a little yeast within three measures of dough, the sower scattering seed in a field, the man digging up a treasure, and the merchant buying and selling pearls. Jesus would often lay his own hands on people in need of healing. On one well-known occasion,

Jesus took up mud and rubbed it into the eyes of a man
who was blind, just as a potter still engaged in his task.

A common observation about leadership, however,
is that it removes people from having to work much
with their hands. Our daily tasks as leaders involve
more visioning and less taking out the trash, more time
managing adults and less time on the playground with
the kids, and more meetings and less changing bedpans
or IVs. The tasks of leadership tend, moreover, to be
highly valued within society and, hence, better paid.
Manual labor is considered "lowly" and some tasks
"beneath us." This is nothing new. The ancient Greeks
understood the life of manual labor as making one
unfit to participate in civic life.[7] And in Jesus's time,
even though Moses and David were celebrated for their
bucolic backgrounds, real shepherds were considered
outcasts because their daily work made it impossible
to keep the cleanliness codes of the religious law.

The perceived division between leadership work
and manual labor, though, serves no one well. If the
early days of the COVID-19 pandemic taught us anything, it is that our lives depend on the manual labor of
those who are often paid the least. The leader who loses
contact with what it is like to work with one's hands
loses connection with those who do and moreover
loses access to much of the gritty reality of the world—
information that is important to have as a leader and
also as a human being. The bifurcation in society at
large becomes mirrored in our own bodies. We run the

risk of losing contact with a constitutive part of what it means to be human in the world.

As Christian leaders, we have always before us the picture of Jesus who, on the night before he died, knelt before his friends wearing an apron and washed the mud from between their toes. And the ritual act of foot washing by the presider at the Holy Thursday service each year reminds us that in Church leadership, no work of the hand is to be considered too lowly for us to be involved in. A bishop who works extensively with the First Nations in Canada relayed to me,

> In indigenous communities, traditionally it was the chief who dug graves. Not the poorest or the weakest, but the leader. The leader always did the most difficult jobs. And leaders were respected because they were willing to do the dirty work, to take on the suffering and grieving. They had authority among the people not because of their title but because they wouldn't ask the people to do something they wouldn't be willing to do themselves.

Sometimes as leaders, though, we will struggle to find a balance in our lives. There are also tasks within organizations that *only* we can do, and there are ways in which we can use the work of the hand as a distraction from what the organization most needs us to be about. It can be tempting to reorganize the church food pantry when we really need to be wrapping our minds around strategic planning. Seeing the pantry in tip-top shape might be more immediately satisfying. How good it feels for many of us to be able to cross something off a list! But there is another work that others depend on us for, and sometimes their ability to be satisfied in their work is contingent on us following through with what is rightly ours.

Furthermore, sometimes the willingness to be involved in all kinds of work manifests itself in micromanaging, which drives everyone that we work alongside bonkers. We forget that much of leadership continues to involve a spirit of "Let there be"—making space for others to exercise their own creativity and know-how in the manner they think best. (More on this in chapter 5!) We need to remember that there is a difference between micromanaging and being "hands on." When micromanaging, we hold on to the power to make every decision while it is often others who carry out the tasks with their hands. When being "hands on," we recognize others have the power of decision-making in their own domains but ask, where we are able, "What can I do with my hands to help?"

Several of the leaders I interviewed indicated that no matter their level of authority within an organization, it was important to them to spend some time each week (or at least each month) working alongside those engaged in manual tasks within the organization— for example, chopping vegetables in the soup kitchen, staying to clean up after the holiday party, or rounding on the hospital floors. Such work helps them get to know people within their organization or community that they might not otherwise get to know and to learn from them as well as build relationships with them. As another bishop shared with me, "I got invited to join the Knights of St. Peter Claver after I served pizza at one of their gatherings. They said they'd never met a bishop who served the pizza before."

Moreover, several leaders noted that beyond their role within the organization, they engage in some kind of hands-on work outside their organization. One pastor in a rural parish had attended community college to be trained as an EMT and joined the volunteer fire department. He claims it helped him to know his town from an angle he would otherwise never have had. Another pastor who serves as a sponsor for those in Alcoholics Anonymous provides occasional temporary lodging in his own home for a person transitioning from life on the street: "It is easy to preach about the importance of caring for one's neighbor from the pulpit. It is much harder when you are holding your neighbor's head up over the toilet because they drank all your hand sanitizer."

Beyond building bridges with others across the power differential or gleaning important insights about wider reality, many leaders noted the importance of regularly engaging in a work of the hand simply for the sake of spiritual groundedness. They observed that gardening, painting, woodworking, or embroidery—even washing dishes and cutting the lawn—helps bring us out of our minds and back into our bodies.

Sometimes after "not thinking" for a while, we will feel our thoughts have become mysteriously clarified, and in physical activity our souls become mysteriously stilled. The connection here can seem tenuous. How does baking a pie help one exercise one's power in more healthy and holy ways as a school principal or director of a foundation? It's hard to say, but we instinctively know there is something about engaging in a "work of the hand" that reconnects us with our fundamental Adam-ness. We are each a creature of the earth shaped by the hands of God, who in turn shapes the earth with our hands. When we work with our hands, we tap into the mystery of our own *b'reisheit*.

Companion for the Journey: **Maria Montessori**

As a child, Maria Montessori hated school. Forced to memorize passages concerning famous women in history, she rebelled. "But you, too, could become famous," her teacher suggested. "Wouldn't you like that?" "Oh no," she replied. "I care too much for the children of the future to add yet another biography to the list."[8] Montessori *did* add another biography, but it would not be a dull one.

Although Montessori was not keen on the classroom, she did enjoy hands-on science and as a teen set her sights on becoming a doctor. With all the odds against her, in 1892, she maneuvered her way into the School of Medicine in Rome—the only woman in the incoming class of 1,664 students. During her studies, Montessori volunteered at a pediatric clinic for the poor where she was exposed to children suffering from malnutrition, tuberculosis, and sexual abuse. Shocked by what she encountered, she decided to focus her practice on psychiatry, particularly the relationship between child-rearing and mental illness.

Following graduation, Montessori became close to a fellow psychiatrist—Giuseppe Montesano—who shared her strong commitment to the poor. When he was named chief physician of the asylum in Rome, she went with him. Together they uncovered the horrific conditions in which patients were housed. Montessori met children with intellectual disabilities who had been permanently locked away in barren rooms. She observed how, after meals, the children crawled on the floor picking up bread crumbs—not out of physical hunger but out of hunger for physical stimulation. What could be done? Montessori began to research the work of two earlier doctors—Jean Marc Gaspard Itard and Édouard Séguin—who had developed hands-on learning materials for such children. She began raising funds to establish schools for the children of the asylum that would employ similar materials.

In the midst of this new endeavor, however, Montessori became pregnant, giving birth to a son, Mario, in March 1898. As a woman at that time in history, her options were severely limited. If she married Montesano, she would no longer be able to practice as a physician and would have to give up her work on behalf of so many children. If she even named Montesano as the father on the birth certificate, she would lose all parental rights. Montessori's mother arranged for Mario to remain a secret and to be raised outside of Rome. For a time, the arrangement held. Montesano and Montessori together founded the Orthophrenic School for the training of teachers to work with children with special needs. But in September 1901, the relationship fell apart. Montesano claimed paternity for Mario and married another woman. Montessori left the Orthophrenic School, devastated.

At this point, Montessori turned to faith in a deeper way. Raised a Catholic, she now began to spend time in silence and spiritual direction. She considered entering a religious community, but the superior of the community instead urged Montessori to pursue her interest in hands-on pedagogy as her vocation: "This method is the work the Lord wants from you."[9]

Montessori began to wonder if what she had learned from Itard and Séguin might be useful in serving children more broadly, not just those with intellectual disabilities. In 1904, she was approached by a social agency working in the impoverished San

Lorenzo district of Rome. While parents were at work in the factories and siblings were in school, the youngest children were often left unattended, wreaking havoc within the housing complexes. Montessori was asked to start kindergartens for the littlest ones. Her former professors from medical school urged her not to give up the prestige and influence she'd earned as one of the first female physicians in Italy to become a preschool director, but Montessori sensed in the invitation a divine call.

On January 6, 1907, Montessori opened the first Casa dei Bambini—or Children's House—in San Lorenzo for fifty children ages two to six years. The teenage daughter of the building custodian served as the lone "teacher." But "teacher" is an ill-suited word here; Montessori never envisioned it as a classroom like those of her own childhood. She wanted to create a space like the Garden of Eden—a carefully prepared environment that the children could joyfully "till and tend" with their own hands. The children were allowed freedom of movement and choice about what material to work with and for how long. The adult would serve as a guide—showing how to use the materials and establishing boundaries to keep the children safe—but the children would learn primarily by "living" in the space. Like Adam, they would exercise their human vocation of dominion in the environment, figuring out how to make it a true home for all gathered there.

The fact that the Children's House was launched on the Feast of Epiphany was not incidental for Montessori. Although it was one small room in a housing project, she opened her own comments that day with Isaiah 60:1: "Arise! Shine, for your light has come!" She later commented, "I don't know what happened to me but I had a vision . . . that the work we were starting would prove to be very important and that one day people would come from all over the world to see it."[10] Montessori's vision was not long in being realized. This work born of the grief of being separated from her own son quickly gave rise to Children's Houses not only in Rome but also across Europe and the United States.

As interest in this new approach to education escalated, Montessori and a handful of her closest followers privately consecrated their lives to God before the altar on Christmas night 1910.[11] That same year she began exploring how the "Montessori method" might be applied to not just reading, writing, science, and math but also religious formation. In Barcelona, she and one of her fellow consecrated colleagues, Anna Maccheroni, created an "atrium"—a sacred space for small children to meet God through hands-on materials related to the Bible and liturgy.

Following the death of her mother in 1912, Montessori was able to reinitiate a relationship with her son Mario, now a young teen. This was a season of healing and joy for Montessori as he came to live with her and became her closest companion. As Montessori published her educational insights and demands for international speaking engagements grew, Mario traveled extensively with her around Europe, the United States, and even India where the two were forced to remain for seven years during the Second World War.

The experience of war made Montessori ever more convinced of a connection between pedagogy and violence. When forced to remain seated at desks and obey the voice of a single teacher in the front of the room who offers rewards and punishments, she realized children were being socialized for the "science of war," whereas she sought a new "science of peace." She wrote extensively about the relationship between pedagogy and peace in her later years and was nominated for the Nobel Peace Prize no fewer than three times.

Montessori died in 1952 at the age of eighty-two. There are now fifteen thousand Montessori schools around the globe, including three thousand in the United States,[12] but there are many more schools that have been influenced by Montessori's emphasis on the work of the hand in human development and learning. Her idea of "atria" for faith formation has also continued to flourish, and such environments now exist in sixty-five countries across multiple Christian traditions.[13] It all began, however, with one woman's desire to use the limited power she had at the turn of

the twentieth century to "give some little children a
chance to live."[14]

For Reflection

- Genesis emphasizes God's "hands-on" role in the
  creation of humanity. Why do you think this was
  important to our ancestors in faith? What is the
  difference for you between "Let there be" and "Let
  us make"?

- The Bible frequently highlights the physical work
  leaders did before taking on leadership roles, as
  if there were an important connection between
  the two. What was your work before taking on
  your current position? How did it prepare you for
  leadership?

- How do you as a leader know when to jump in and
  get involved in the physical work that allows your
  community to function? What are the clues that
  indicate to you that you instead need to prioritize
  other tasks?

- Do you have a work of the hand that you continue
  to enjoy? What do you see as being the fruits of this
  labor in your life?

- What insight do you glean from Maria Montessori's
  story concerning the spirituality of power?

2. Exercising the Power to Speak

God said: Let there be light, and there was light. God saw that the light was good. God then separated the light from the darkness. God called the light "day," and the darkness he called "night." Evening came, and morning followed—the first day.

—Genesis 1:3–5

So the LORD God formed out of the ground all the wild animals and all the birds of the air, and he brought them to the man to see what he would call them; whatever the man called each living creature was then its name. The man gave names to all the tame animals, all the birds of the air, and all the wild animals; but none proved to be a helper suited to the man.

—Genesis 2:19–20

In the beginning of Genesis, there are no dragons. There are no bloody battles. There are words—powerful words—and each time one of these words is spoken, something else comes into being, each with its own name: Day, Night, Sky, Earth, and Sea. In the ancient world, names were tremendously significant. It was almost as if a thing did not exist before it had a name. Names were understood to reveal something important about a creature's nature. Parents might wait months or even years to give a child a name, until they felt they knew their child's unique traits or personality. And even then, one would keep one's given name secret from strangers. To let a person know your name—perhaps like giving out your cell phone number today—was to give them some degree of power over you.[1] As noted in the *Catechism of the Catholic Church*, "To disclose one's name is to make oneself known to others; in a way it is to hand oneself over by becoming accessible, capable of being known more intimately and addressed personally" (203).

The power of speaking, and naming in particular, is a power explicitly shared with humans in the second story of creation. God brings the many animals of the earth to the human being to see what the human will call them, and the names given become their names. It is interesting to consider how this activity again mirrors what we are coming to understand about the acquisition of language in human development. As we talked about in chapter 1, the first way that we begin to communicate is with our hands in the form of gestures. Then in toddlerhood, as Maria Montessori went on to

observe, we become fascinated with nomenclature—
the discovery of names—and, intriguingly, animal
names still comprise a disproportionate percentage of
the vocabulary of young children.[2]

There are many ways to understand the relationship that Genesis 2:19 establishes between the human
and animal world. As noted above, giving a name is
an act of honoring another. It acknowledges the other's
existence. It implies an act of discernment; *adam* can't
give a name without knowing something of the nature
of the other. *Adam* is like a parent to the animals; they
are all family. At the same time, naming in itself is an
act of power over another. As with revealing one's
name to another, being named by another implies the
other has access to you, but even more so has some
power to define your identity, to craft how you might
even come to see yourself. It is only later in the story,
after the incident with the snake, that Adam (now likely
intended as a proper name rather than a reference to
humanity in general) names the woman Eve—"the
mother of all the living" (Gn 3:20). Is this a description
of how he has come to know her, honoring her true
self? Or is this an act of power over her that defines
her role forevermore? Naming is a messy, complicated
business.

That messiness extends to speech in general. Every
act of speech in some way is an act of naming[3]—not
necessarily for the first time as with *adam* in the garden,
but every time a word is repeated it reinforces the

relationship we have with that object or creature, and not without consequence. The way we classify someone shapes what we notice and how we respond to them. If I hear someone is a "bully" versus "a person who is wounded," I am likely to treat them quite differently, even though they are the same person. If someone calls me "girl" even though I am now in my fifties, there is a good chance I will feel stuck in the role of a nine-year-old during the conversation that follows.

We name not only some ones and some things but also some times. We are constantly narrating our understanding of events in our day and events in the past. Every story we tell includes some information about what happened and excludes other facts. It interprets what those events mean, and the words we choose influence how we and those around us look at the world. Later in this chapter, we will meet Nicholas Black Elk, who at the age of ten participated in what the Lakota people call the Battle of the Greasy Grass, an event that I was taught as a child to call Custer's Last Stand. As an adult, Black Elk lived through what I learned to call the Battle of Wounded Knee but is now referred to often as the Massacre at Wounded Knee. The difference can seem subtle, but where we put the spotlight in our naming determines what we see. In this sense, every act of speech is an act of power. It continues to create the world that we live in and to assert some knowledge of its nature. What a wondrous thing! And what a responsibility.

To complicate matters further, not everyone's words carry an equal impact. The words of some disproportionately influence the thoughts and actions of others. This magnified influence is often linked to institutional roles. "I was so confused the first couple of meetings I held," a new director of Catholic Charities told me.

> I would toss an idea out casually trying to elicit others' ideas, and everyone immediately moved to action as if I had given a command. It only became clear to me why when I had my first meeting with the archdiocesan attorneys. They told me, "The way that the bylaws are written, if the whole board votes to go right and you say, 'Let's go left,' then we will go left." No wonder everyone was taking my words so seriously.

For others, the magnified influence comes from not a job title but an artful command of language mingled with luck. A Christian social media influencer told me of a poem that she wrote early in the pandemic. When she posted it online, it went viral. "I was interviewed on TV," she said.

> The poem was translated into other languages. I got thousands of followers from it. On one hand, I can acknowledge I worked hard on this; I've spent a lot of time studying my craft. But at the same time, it has been a bewildering experience. People

started following me without even knowing who
I am or what I care about.

In such circumstances, it is even *more* difficult to know
how to manage responsibly the power of one's speech.

Jesus was one who clearly had a way with words.
Although he had no institutional role, he was a master
communicator. There was genuine craft to his preaching
too—whether it was his short, easy-to-remember
maxims such as those found in the Sermon on the
Mount or his many parables.[4] And surely, he worked
hard to hone his skills. But his message about the reign
of God certainly went viral, drawing crowds wherever
he went. Was it a bewildering experience for him too?
Did he ever struggle with the magnified impact of his
words? Did he say things in good humor that others
took as law? Hard to know. What we do know is that
people began to regard him as a *parrhesiastes*.[5]

To call anyone a *parrhesiastes* could raise eyebrows.
Parrhesia sounds like something that Jesus would have
healed rather than enjoyed. But parrhesia in Jesus's
time was a source of both awe and envy. The term
comes from Greek culture and means the freedom to
speak boldly, plainly, and truthfully. Parrhesia was
most associated with ancient Athens where citizens
treasured their right to speak their minds—even about
government leaders—without fear of punishment.[6] In
the colonies of Rome, speaking one's mind involved far
more risk. This is because, throughout the Greco-Roman

world, parrhesia was a freedom associated with power. Those with social status, such as the citizens of Athens, had the freedom to be frank. Those without social status, such as Jewish peasants, did not.

Contemporary psychology continues to document the relationship between parrhesia and power. Each of us has a gap between what we think in our minds and what comes out of our mouths. For those of us who see ourselves as having less power, even today, that gap will likely be quite large as the consequences for speaking up are more pronounced and hence more vivid in the imagination. For those of us who see ourselves as having more power, even today, that gap will likely be smaller, as we have less fear that we will suffer for speaking up. Indeed, research indicates that persons who experience power are less socially inhibited overall. They are more likely to dress as they please, speak with less filter, and take up more space in the conversation.[7] As with the classic chicken-egg scenario, it can be difficult to sort which came first: Do people who speak boldly tend to gain power? Or is it that people who have power no longer have to worry about filtering their thoughts? All we can say is that—then as now—parrhesia and power are deeply intertwined.

What made Jesus such an oddity was that he exhibited parrhesia even without the normal accoutrements of power that would protect him from suffering negative consequences. He spoke frankly and publicly even though he did not come from a wealthy family or have a position in government. He exhibited no fear, even though those around him could see the possible danger. Listening to him preach must have been like watching a tightrope walker without a net: thrilling and terrifying at the same time. The crowds couldn't pull their eyes away. Parrhesia magnified his power. At the same time, he was exercising a power commonly understood to be reserved for those "with power," so his parrhesia also made him vulnerable. Parrhesiastes "without power" easily become pariahs.

As Christian leaders, we know that like Jesus we are called to be people who speak boldly, plainly, and truthfully. We want to be honest and courageous in using the power of language to speak a new world into being. Not through the slaying of dragons but by words do we also do our part in building up the reign of God. One of the greatest failures in life, we often realize too late, is *not* speaking up publicly about grave injustices in our society—and even grave injustices in our own institutions—because we are afraid of what the consequences to our own selves might be. Fearful that we don't have "enough power" to avoid retribution, we don't embrace the power that we *do* have to name what is in front of us.

In 2002, a handful of us in Church ministry found ourselves like the crowds on the hillside in Israel—simultaneously in awe of and nervous for the young lay chancellor of a rural diocese who boldly read aloud a ten-page letter he'd written to his bishop, then the head of the US Conference of Catholic Bishops, challenging the bishops' leadership on the sexual abuse crisis.[8] His example of parrhesia—the story of which only slowly became public in national news—helped to shape the Church's zero-tolerance policy for sexual abuse. And it forced many of us to wonder: Do I have that kind of courage? For what would I be willing to lose my job? What keeps me from being bolder in situations where I see others in harm's way? At the same time, one cannot ignore the bishop's role in this story. He heard the challenge, acted on the feedback, and then continued to foster an atmosphere in which coworkers could dare boldness. Indeed, two decades later, and two dioceses later, the two men continue to work with each other.

As Christian leaders, perhaps an even greater challenge than *being* a parrhesiastes is creating the kind of culture that honors others' parrhesia. We are aware of how hard it is for each of us to speak up to power; we are often unaware that others may be struggling to speak up to us. The "higher" we are in the hierarchy of an organization, the greater degree of freedom we will naturally feel in sharing our own thoughts in meetings. We may even become befuddled why others don't assert themselves more. Why don't they just speak up if they have something to say? The exercise of holy power requires extra attentiveness on our part regarding just how much we say and when. "Even if

I think I'm just one more voice at the table, I need to remember I'm not," several leaders told me. "If I want brainstorming at a meeting, I'll have to make sure I'm the last one to throw an idea out," said one. Another noted, "I've learned that I need to have one-on-one meetings before big meetings because people are more willing to challenge my ideas in private whereas they won't in front of the large group."

The exercise of holy power also demands extra care in choosing the words we use when we do speak. Church father Gregory the Great drew attention to this challenge already in the year 600 when writing about St. Benedict (whom we will meet in the next chapter). "Even his common speech was not devoid of spiritual weight," Gregory observed, "because when a person's heart is focused on heavenly matters, his words never tumble useless from his mouth. If he said anything threatening but without considering it, his word had so much power that it was as if he had uttered a verdict and not spoken tentatively."[9] Note that Gregory wasn't saying Benedict's casual comments were malicious, only that because Benedict had so much power—in this case the power of spiritual authenticity—even his casual comments had an unintended impact and hence required heightened attention. In the words of a current bishop whom I interviewed, "I've learned that words I've meant as pebbles in a pond have sometimes landed like asteroids."

Such meticulous care of language can be exhausting and sometimes overwhelming. Who among us has not received an email letting us know that a particular term we used in a speech was not inclusive or that the language shared in an announcement was offensive to someone? Off-the-cuff remarks and humor can become particularly dicey. "I can remember early on," relayed a former seminary rector,

> I was joking with one of the seminarians who was a very fun guy. I was busting his chops on a couple of things in 100 percent jest. He came a week later and asked, "Monsignor, have I done something wrong? I feel like you've been riding me lately." That was the day I realized the rector is not anybody's friend, at least certainly isn't anybody's buddy.

It is hard when ways that we've previously used to connect casually now unintentionally cause another hurt. We should be gentle with ourselves as we strive to accept responsibility for the heightened impact of our words. The power of language is one of the greatest powers God has shared with us. We are all still trying to figure it out.

Companion for the Journey: **Nicholas Black Elk**

Like Jesus, Nicholas Black Elk came of age in a time of unspeakable oppression and misery. Born along the Wyoming-Montana border in 1866, Black Elk's early years were marked by war, broken treaties, the decimation of the buffalo, and the forced settlement of his people—the Oglala Lakota—onto the Pine Ridge Indian Reservation of South Dakota. Yet, also like Jesus, Black Elk found needed meaning and hope in the spiritual tradition of his people.

Black Elk did not grow up with stories of Adam and Eve, but at the age of nine, during a life-threatening illness, he experienced a vision that strangely echoes Genesis. He saw a council of grandfathers placing a tree of life in the center of the world. "They put the stick into the center of the hoop," he recalled, "And you could hear birds singing all kinds of songs by this flowering stick and the people and animals all rejoiced and hollered."[10] In this vision, the grandfathers gifted him with powers necessary for the care and healing of his people. He knew he was called to become a medicine man.

During Black Elk's teen and young adult years, he continued to experience visions that helped him embrace his call. He spent two years traveling the eastern United States and Europe with "Buffalo Bill" Cody's Wild West troupe. "[I thought] maybe if I could see the great world of the Wasichu (White Man), I could understand how to bring the sacred hoop together and make the tree bloom again at the center of it," he later reflected.[11] But when Black Elk returned to the Pine Ridge Reservation in 1888, the desperation of his people was greater than ever. Across the Plains, indigenous peoples were embracing the Ghost Dance—a ritual intended to "dance a new world into being"[12] void of the suffering that the Wasichu had brought. While participating in the Ghost Dance himself, Black Elk experienced yet another vision of the sacred tree from his childhood, now in full bloom with a man standing before it with outstretched arms and wounds in the palms of his hands. Black Elk later noted this was the moment he began to identify Jesus as the "chief" who could make the tree bloom fully.[13]

Frightened by the Ghost Dance ritual and the surge of hope it evoked across the reservation, skirmishes between the Lakota and the US military increased, leading to a devastating event at Wounded Knee Creek on December 29, 1890, in which between 150 and 300 Lakota—many unarmed women and children—died. Black Elk, who arrived on the scene shortly after the killing had taken place, carried the scars of this event for the rest of his life.

It was in this same period, however, that Jesuit priests arrived in Pine Ridge at the request of Lakota chief Red Cloud. Red Cloud saw the rituals of the Sina Sapa ("Blackrobes") as similar to those of his

medicine men and requested they build a school on
the reservation. Black Elk had close relationships
with several Catholic Lakota—including Katie War
Bonnet, whom he married in 1892 and with whom he
had three children before her death in 1901. He also
struck up friendships with several of the Jesuit priests.
On December 6, 1904, Black Elk chose to be baptized,
taking the name *Nicholas* in honor of the saint of the
day who was also known as a generous healer. For
the remainder of his life, he would be known by those
closest to him as "Nick."

It is perplexing to many how a man whose life and
culture had been decimated by encounters with the
"Christian world" could choose to become Christian
himself, but Black Elk did not see his Baptism as a
break from his Lakota spiritual heritage. Like Red
Cloud, he saw the two traditions as compatible and
that, indeed, his Lakota way of practicing Christianity
was a challenge to the Wasichu who did not live the
values considered central to their faith. As he would
later preach with parrhesia to a largely white assembly
in 1913, "You came to this country which was ours in
the first place. We were the only inhabitants. . . . But
you're not doing what you're supposed to do—
what our religion and our Bible tells us. I know this.
Christ himself preached that we love our neighbor as
ourselves. Do unto others as you would have others
do unto you."[14]

Shortly after his Baptism, Black Elk married his second wife, Anna Brings White, with whom he would have two more children. He also began working as a catechist. This role involved educating children in the Christian faith. Black Elk loved children and enjoyed showing them his "Two Roads Map," an illustrated biblical history of salvation. But serving as a catechist at that time also involved the pastoral leadership of a local community—visiting the sick, preaching, leading prayer, coordinating gatherings, fundraising, baptizing babies, and burying the dead. Black Elk was primarily responsible for the St. Agnes Church community in Manderson, South Dakota, and his home with Anna served as a sort of pastoral center. Black Elk also frequently traveled to speak in other communities. "When he got up, he really preached," an interview with a Manderson parishioner revealed. "People sat there and just listened to him. They could picture what he was talking about."[15] A Jesuit traveling companion wrote, "On a moment's notice he can pour forth a flood of oratory holding his hearers spellbound. There are few that can resist him and none of whom he is afraid."[16] Over four hundred people embraced Christianity through Black Elk's teaching and preaching.

Later in life, Black Elk's bold and challenging voice reached even further through the publication of *Black Elk Speaks*, the fruit of an interview with poet John Niehardt, and *The Sacred Pipe*, emerging out of interviews with scholar Joseph Epes Brown. These texts, which focused more on his early life history and the preservation of Lakota spiritual traditions, give little attention to his active Christian ministry, but his Christian beliefs are nevertheless integrated into so many of his comments. "We live under the flowering stick like under the wing of a hen," he says in allusion to the Cross.[17]

Nicholas Black Elk died a revered Lakota elder and Catholic pastoral leader on August 17, 1950. He is buried at the St. Agnes cemetery in Manderson, with a simple wooden cross behind his hand-chiseled tombstone. In 2017, at the request of several of Black Elk's descendants, his cause for canonization was opened. Someday soon the Church may have a Lakota saint to celebrate on its calendar. Meanwhile—through his books, letters, and preaching notes—Black Elk's bold and visionary words continue to challenge us all.

For Reflection

- One of the first and weightiest powers that God explicitly shares with humans in Genesis is the power to name. What memories from your own life do you associate with "naming"? Who or what have you been able to name?

- Have there been moments in your time as a leader that awakened you to the particular power of your words compared to others' words? What was it like for you to discover your words held such great weight?

- What guidelines have you established for yourself as a leader about when to speak up and how? Can you think of any times that you wished you'd spoken up sooner? Times you wish you'd waited to speak?

- To what do you credit Jesus's freedom to speak without fear, even as there were so many potential bad consequences for doing so?

- What insight do you glean from Nicholas Black Elk's story concerning the spirituality of power, especially the power of speech?

3. Exercising the Power to Order

God said: Let there be a dome in the middle of the waters, to separate one body of water from the other. God made the dome, and it separated the water below the dome from the water above the dome. And so it happened. God called the dome "sky." Evening came, and morning followed—the second day. Then God said: Let the water under the sky be gathered into a single basin, so that the dry land may appear. And so it happened: the water under the sky was gathered into its basin, and the dry land appeared. God called the dry land "earth," and the basin of water he called "sea." God saw that it was good. Then God said: Let the earth bring forth vegetation: every kind of plant that bears seed and every kind of fruit tree on earth that bears fruit with its seed in it. And so it happened: the earth brought forth vegetation: every kind of plant that bears seed and every kind of fruit tree that bears fruit with its seed in it. God saw that

it was good. Evening came, and morning
followed—the third day.

—Genesis 1:6–13

For those who glory in the work of administration,
the first story of creation in Genesis is a cause for awe.
During the first three days, God ever so carefully
prepares three environments: separating light from
darkness, the water below from the water above,
and then the land from the sea. During the second
set of three days, God now populates each of these
environments. On day four, the light and darkness
receive the sun, moon, and stars. On day five, the sky
above is filled with birds and the water below with sea
monsters and every kind of water creature. On day six,
the dry land is filled with cattle, creeping things, and
wild animals . . . and then finally humans.

The gorgeous orderliness of it all could make one's
spine tingle. Each element of creation builds on what
has come before. Humans could not flourish without
animals who could not flourish without plants who
could not flourish without land and who rely on water
and light. This first story of creation presents us with a
God who is "on top of things." A God who has a well-
organized plan and knows how to stick to it. A God
who can kick back on day seven and enjoy how well it
all functions together. Someday, in my exercise of the
human vocation, I would like to successfully imitate

this God. Fortunately, in the meantime, there is the face of God we meet in Genesis 2.

The second story of creation is a source of much consolation for those who are of a more spontaneous ilk. For here we meet a God who at first seems a little disorganized. This God creates a human from the ground of the earth but then finds there is nothing for the human to eat and so plants a garden that still requires a bit of work. God then realizes that the human is alone and so forms animals and birds, but none is a true partner. God does not give up. God instead takes a rib from the human. And now all is well, until . . . it once again isn't.

In this second story of creation, we meet a God who "goes with the flow," a God who is responsive to each need as it arises, and a God who is always on call. Is one way of "being God"—and hence, imitating God— better than the other? Not necessarily. As Catholics in leadership, both organization and flexibility will be asked of us.

In Jesus's life, this was certainly true. In his teaching, Jesus urges people to plan appropriately and know what they are getting into before they leap. He challenges us to not build houses on sand, but on rock (Mt 7:24–27). He says to first sit down and estimate the cost before building a tower (Lk 14:28). He questions what king goes out to battle without knowing how many troops his opponent has (Lk 14:31).

And early in the gospels, we meet a Jesus who seems to have taken his own advice. He goes into the desert for forty days and emerges with a clear understanding of who he is and what he is to be about. He intentionally chooses twelve disciples to follow him closely, a sign that he has come to reunite the "twelve tribes of Israel"—his own people who have become divided and scattered from one another. When he sends them out to preach, he instructs them to go not to Gentile or Samaritan towns but "to the lost sheep of the house of Israel" (Mt 10:6). When a Canaanite woman calls after him, he reiterates the plan: "I was sent only to the lost sheep of the house of Israel" (Mt 15:24). But this does not go well as she refuses to depart and begs him to shift his plan to include her family's needs as well.

And Jesus does. Over and over again. A need presents itself, and he has to pivot. He tries preaching, but then someone rips off the roof to let down a paralyzed friend. He returns from a trip only to discover a desperate Jairus waiting at the dock, but on the way to Jairus's home, he is halted again by a hemorrhaging woman in need of help. It almost seems as if the only trip Jesus took that went as expected was his final one to Jerusalem.

One of the primary job descriptions of any leader is to "bring order out of chaos," and yet chaos seems mighty determined to continue to reassert itself. In the first story of creation—and indeed throughout much of Hebrew Scripture—chaos is represented by the primordial waters present from the very first verse of Genesis. It is similar in other Mesopotamian myths as well. The primordial sea represents the unknown, the mysterious, the murky. In Mesopotamian mythology, this sea is deified and personalized as "Tiamat," the goddess slayed and split in two by the god Marduk to form the heavens and the earth.

Biblical scholar Jon Levenson argues that in Genesis, God never entirely conquers the waters of chaos as happens in other myths from the region. Rather, God sets boundaries on the water, some held back by the dome of the sky and some held in place by the shorelines of the sea. But as exemplified in the story of Noah, the waters still sometimes break through. "In Genesis 1," he says, "the waters have been . . . neutralized . . . demythologized . . . even depersonalized. They have not, however, been eliminated."[1] Tiamat—in the Bible called *Leviathan*—has not been slayed. The reining in of chaos is not a onetime event but something that God is engaged in every day, a work not yet finished. God's mastery is often fragile, Levenson asserts, "in continual need of reactivation and reassertion and at times, as in the laments, painfully distant from ordinary experience, a memory and a hope rather than a current reality."[2]

Our experience as Christian leaders often mirrors God's challenge. For my first twenty years in administration, I kept saying, "As soon as I get my act together, I will . . ." Then I finally realized I was never going to get my act together once and for all. Indeed, last year I realized I may not even have an "act." The attempt, however, matters.

As leaders, we are the ones who largely construct the environments in which others work. When we use our power to do that organizational work well—when there are good policies in place, when meetings have agendas, when emails are answered and requests are processed promptly, and when people know where to turn to get clarity on next steps—the people who work with us can do their own work and live their own lives in a relatively orderly and sane fashion. But often this kind of work is not particularly glamorous. "My favorite passage in the whole Bible," the chancellor of a diocese told me, "is the one about not going into battle without first checking out your troops." He continued:

> At the chancery office, the bishop wanted to make a change in the way that the diocesan appeal was run. But to do that without causing utter chaos, first we had to create a diocesan database, which meant getting all the parishes to use the same software, which required quite a financial outlay. Making what looked like a simple change took five years of step-by-step planning. But when we skimp on that kind of planning behind the scenes, craziness ensues—not just for the chancery staff but for all the parish staffs too.

Sometimes leaders will say, "I'm a big picture person. I'm not good at returning emails," and then shrug as if those around them should learn to live with this reality. But there is an ethical dimension to such a claim. The way we choose to use our energy, and in particular, the way we choose to use our time, is in itself an exercise of power. Leadership is tough. It makes many demands, and it often feels as if our time is no longer our own. Much happens that we legitimately cannot control. And yet, if we are chronically busy and impossible to reach, if people can't get the answers from us that they need to move forward with the projects they are working on, and if others are constantly tasked with putting out our fires or scrambling at the last minute because we decided to build a tower without first making sure we had the construction supplies, it is not just we who struggle but others even more so.

When we are honest about it, yes, sometimes the unexpected happens, but many times the chaos that reigns in a workplace is not due to Leviathan so much as an inability on the part of us leaders to manage ourselves. We chronically say yes to more than we can do, even if with the best of intentions. We neglect to leave any margin for the unanticipated, even if years of life experience have taught us that there *will* be something we've not anticipated. We underestimate the impact of our own hectic schedule on the lives of those who work most closely with us, even though they've given us this feedback in myriad ways.

These patterns often are excused in our culture because lack of responsiveness is an accepted behavior for those who are busy and busyness is read as an indication of importance. But eventually, we must acknowledge that no matter how well-meaning we are, we are participating in a power play. We are communicating, "My time is more valuable than yours. It is okay that my lack of order means your life can't have order." This is a misuse of dominion, which is always intended to be used so that others beyond oneself can live in peace and harmony.

Leaders committed to a healthy and holy exercise of power are willing to give time to the sometimes less gratifying, less exciting tasks of organizing, planning, and structuring, which others might not see—indeed, might take for granted. Leaders committed to a healthy and holy exercise of power will also be intentional about organizing their own lives in such a way that they do not regularly impinge upon others' capacity to keep some degree of order in theirs. Seeking spiritual direction, receiving coaching, or having an accountability partner are all good ways of working with our own internal waters of chaos, which we will never be entirely rid of but can learn how to set boundaries on.

On the other extreme, we have all likely met (or in my case, been) leaders who love orderliness to such a degree that they become inflexible: persons who are unable to be responsive to change in the moment and demand that the world at all times continues to conform to their plan. This stance, too, presents an ethical challenge. It pretends that chaos has once and for all already been conquered—that God's organizational task and our own have already been completed, and now people must just "get with the program." Such leaders can lack mercy before the reality of Leviathan's ongoing existence in others' lives, and even their own. Often, those most adamant about not cutting others any slack are also extremely hard on themselves, and vice versa.

In interviews, many leaders told me that if they hear the word *pivot* one more time this decade, they will retreat to a cave more remote than Benedict's at Subiaco (see below) to take up a hermit's existence. And yet they know that their best-laid plans must still be held with a certain degree of detachment. As leaders, we prepare, we anticipate, we are proactive about what we see coming, and we build in margins. We plan to stay the course. Yet sometimes we do have to change course. We adapt. To be rigid about rules and committed to processes more than the people these processes intend to serve is also a poor exercise of dominion.

And so, we continue to seek the holy in-between space in which we form the best environments we can with the power we have. Environments that are ordered for life to flourish and in which it is easy to do one's best work. But we know that creating such environments is an art more than a science. Despite

all the advice that books on management offer, there
are no hard-and-fast rules applicable in every context.
We practice planning as we embrace the unknown.
We create policies knowing they have exceptions. We
strive for order while understanding that sometimes
the waters will still burst through.

Companion for the Journey: **Benedict of Nursia**

What little we know about the life of Benedict comes
from a series of stories recorded by Pope Gregory the
Great around fifty years after Benedict's death in AD
547. Gregory introduces Benedict as a young adult
leaving his home in the Umbrian mountain town
now known as Norcia to pursue higher education in
Rome. Dismayed by the dissolute lifestyle of fellow
classmates, Gregory notes that Benedict departed the
city shortly after he arrived "learnedly ignorant and
wisely uninstructed."[3] With the help of a monk named
Romulus, he found a cave in Subiaco about forty miles
east of the city, where he spent three years as a hermit
before his presence and reputed holiness began to draw
visitors in his direction.

A group of monks in nearby Vicovaro sought him
out as their leader after their own leader died. Benedict
reluctantly consented but was alarmed when he saw
how chaotic their community's life was. Even at this
early stage of monasticism, it was expected Christians

who wanted to devote themselves to prayer as a member of a community would have some sort of "rule of life" everyone agreed to in order to work and pray with one another in harmony.

There were several such rules already in existence, for example, the Rule of St. Augustine, the Rule of St. Basil, and the Rule of the Master. Often these rules were very strict, establishing a life of extreme asceticism, which was difficult to sustain over the long haul. The community in Vicovaro had grown lax in following its rule and Benedict tried to call them back to a more rigorous observance of the practices they had signed onto. It seems that Benedict himself may have been quite a stickler for making sure rules were followed. He irritated the monks so greatly that at one point they tried to poison his drink. Suffice it to say Benedict's first attempt at leadership did not go well.

Benedict returned to Subiaco and to his hermit's life, but visitors continued to arrive, including a growing number of young men who wanted to join him in his life of prayer. Benedict formed not one but *twelve* monasteries along the steep hillside of Subiaco overlooking a lake. Each of the monasteries had twelve monks, mirroring Jesus's gathering of the twelve disciples. In 1516, he wrote his own rule of life for these communities.

The Rule of Benedict is seventy-three chapters long, which makes it sound as if it would be overbearing, but Benedict's chapters are quite short.

Indeed, his entire rule is one-third the length of the
Rule of the Master. Perhaps having learned from his
experience at Vicovaro, he proposes a more moderate
form of communal life with the monastery as a "school
for the service of God in which we hope nothing harsh
nor burdensome will be ordained."[4]

Benedict organizes his community around an
abbot chosen not for his charisma but for his spiritual
maturity and managerial skills. The final word on
matters resides with the abbot, but a variety of other
community roles are outlined as well: the cellarer who
makes sure community property is distributed among
the monks as needed, the doorkeeper to greet guests,
the novice master who initiates new members, and a
dean for each group of ten monks.

Everyone is to take a turn in the kitchen. In matters
involving the whole community, the abbot calls them
all together to give counsel, paying special attention
to the insights of the youngest monks, "because the
Lord often reveals to the younger what is best."[5] In less
important matters, the abbot consults the senior monks.
The newest and oldest members of the community are
to be treated with particular gentleness.

Parts of Benedict's rule now seem odd, for
example, the regulation not to sleep with one's knife.[6]
But Benedict's communities welcomed men from
many different socioeconomic classes, cultures, and
generations. As evident in Gregory's stories, the earliest
members at Subiaco included children of Roman

noblemen as well as Goths. Benedict was trying to organize a way for fellow Christians to live together in community in peace. Sometimes things one might take for granted need to be made explicit.

And it worked. For 1,500 years now, Benedict's rule has served as a way of organizing life in both men's and women's communities around the globe. Perhaps this is because the Rule expects from the beginning that all will *not* go as planned. Several chapters deal with what to do when community members violate the Rule or circumstances make it challenging to keep. In the stories that Gregory tells, the humanity of the monks is a constant: One struggles with pride at being asked to do a task he feels beneath him. Another is stingy in sharing the community's oil. But even beyond the monks, life deals in the unexpected. In Gregory's tales, the lake at Subiaco seems to play a role like that of the chaotic waters in the story of creation: nearly drowning one beloved monk and stealing a valuable tool from another. Benedict's rule never imagines order as something established once and for all. It is a fragile thing that needs ongoing tending and repeated repair.

Toward the end of his life, though, Benedict learned one last important lesson about life in community. By this time, he had departed Subiaco to form yet another monastery on the hilltop above the town of Cassino, about seventy miles to the southeast. The new location put him near his sister Scholastica, abbess of a women's monastery in Piumarola. The two would meet annually at an in-between location.

On one occasion she begged him to stay longer, but he insisted that the Rule demanded his return to the monastery by nightfall. Scholastica bent her head in prayer, and although it had been a sunny day, torrential rain began to fall. In Gregory's account, Benedict exclaims, "What have you done?!" and Scholastica replies, "Look, I asked you and you wouldn't listen. So I asked my Lord and he listened." Benedict spent the night in continued conversation with Scholastica before returning to the monastery in the morning. Three days later she died. "After a long period of progress in personal and legislative discipline," says one commentator on this story, "Benedict had reached a stage where he needed a lesson in love [from his sister]. The Rule had taken him as far as it could, and now he needed to give himself over to love. . . . At this final stage of his maturity, the great legislator needed to become like a little child again."[7] The Rule was created to serve the community; the community was not created to serve the Rule.

For Reflection

- Are you more attracted to the picture of God gleaned from the first story of creation or the second? Do you have a sense as to why?

- Which is the greater danger for you: being too structured or not structured enough? What feedback have you received from others regarding this trait? How do you see your own tendency affecting the ability of others to live sane lives?

- What clues do you find in the gospels about Jesus's balance of order and flexibility in his ministry?

- Do you agree with the assertion that the way we manage our time is inherently an exercise of power and that lack of organization can be just as much a form of power abuse as instituting too much structure?

- What insight do you glean from the life of Benedict of Nursia concerning what it means to live power in a holy and healthy way, particularly in the arena of "order"?

4. Exercising the Power to Convene

> Then God said: Let us make human beings in our image, after our likeness. Let them have dominion over the fish of the sea, the birds of the air, the tame animals, all the wild animals, and all the creatures that crawl on the earth. God created mankind in his image; in the image of God he created them; male and female he created them.
>
> —Genesis 1:26–27

Few passages of scripture have elicited more ink than the mysterious phrase at the heart of Genesis 1:26: *Naaseh*. "Let us make." Generation upon generation of commentators have hypothesized who this "us" might be. Is it simply an instance of the "royal we," the way kings and queens and persons of great power are apt to speak? Is it a very early revelation of God as Trinity, as some of the church fathers like Augustine of Hippo and Gregory of Nyssa believed?

In Jewish commentary, it is most often thought that God was speaking to the heavenly court of angels. "Since Man was to be in the likeness of the angels and they would be jealous of him, He consulted them. . . . He asked permission of His court," suggested the famous eleventh-century rabbi known as Rashi. "In spite of the license given to heretics by this formulation, the text does not restrain itself from teaching the virtue of humility: the *great* one should consult with, request permission from the *small* one."[1]

The eighteenth-century rabbi Vilna Gaon, however, understood the mysterious "us" as referring to God and the world. He envisioned God addressing all of the creatures that had already come into being, "bidding each to contribute a portion of its characteristics to man. For man's strength is traced to the lion; his swiftness to the eagle; his cunning to the fox; his capacity for growth to the flora; and his living soul to the living beings—all of which are harmonized within man."[2]

Whichever of the above best reflects the mind of the text's author, the phrase gives us an important insight into our human nature: We were created within the context of an "us"—a convening. And if we are made in the image and likeness of this utterly relational God, this God-who-gathers, then we, too, must be those-who-gather.

Jesus's ministry reflects this reality. As noted in chapter 3, Jesus launches his ministry by calling together twelve disciples representing the twelve ancient "tribes of Israel" who over the course of their history had become separated from one another. He understands his overarching mission as gathering his people, fashioning them into an "us" again.

Throughout his ministry, Jesus seems to never want to miss a potential party. As far as we know, he participates in every convening he is invited to, which often means being the guest of honor around a dinner table. He eats with sinners and tax collectors. He also eats at the home of Simon the Pharisee. His willingness to gather with whoever asks him is criticized by those who see convening as condoning, yet he understands these meals as symbolic of this larger work he is about, bringing together people who might not ordinarily ever talk with one another, much less eat with one another. These gatherings were for him a foreshadowing of the reign of God that he preached about. And more than a foreshadowing, these gatherings were a way to help bring that day about.

When an invitation to gather was not forthcoming quickly enough, Jesus was not opposed to inviting himself to another's table: "Zaccheus," he said, "today I must stay at your house" (Lk 19:5). In the Temple, he overturned the tables where money was exchanged, tables that had become divisive and exclusive, making it difficult for the poor to worship alongside the wealthy. And on the night before he died, of course, Jesus himself convened a final gathering, playing the roles of host and servant and meal. He commanded that now we continue to do so, in memory of him.

The power to convene is one of the most fundamental ways every human is called to exercise dominion. It is a power exercised every hour of every day wherever families eat dinner, friends meet for coffee, committee meetings are held, and Zoom conferences are organized. It is such a treasured power that it is enshrined in many national constitutions: the right to gather with one another and the right to call people together. And yet, even within this most basic human dynamic, there exist power differentials: the capacity of some to convene is greater than others. Not everyone is equally invited to the table. Not everyone feels daring enough to invite themselves. Not everyone can imagine themselves in the role of the host. Not all who call people together will get a response. People with "power over" find it easier to get a place at the table, and perhaps even more important, they find it easier to do the inviting.

"I had a new insight when watching the funeral of Queen Elizabeth II," one school administrator shared with me:

> The news commentators were talking about what kind of power she had. Politically it wasn't much. England has a prime minister and all. But one mentioned that her greatest power was actually the power to convene people. When the queen invited you to something, you showed up. And I realized that this is actually the greatest power I have in my role as the curriculum chair at my

school as well. When I call a meeting, people tend
to show up. Others can call meetings, but everyone
might not come.

When we talked about why this was, she acknowledged
that certainly part of it came from her institutional
role: She can write evaluative comments on faculty
performance reviews. But faculty are not the only
ones who will show up when she calls. She believes
that part of others' willingness to gather comes from
her commitment to that age-old tradition of providing
food. She continued, "My grandma would say, 'No
one will come if you don't feed them.' I think of Jesus
saying, 'I am the one who feeds you. I am the bread
of life.' That is a motivating scripture for me. I feed
them, and they listen to me more readily because I've
fed them." "My hope," she concluded, "is that I'm
using my power well, that the table becomes a place
of belonging."

Her hope was one shared by many of the leaders
I spoke with, and one that they pondered a great deal:
Yes, we have the power to gather people, and yes, we
have a heightened chance of people showing up, but
how best to then exercise this power? Whom should
we be calling to the table and for what purpose? How
can we learn from more voices? How can we widen the
sense of belonging and participating? How can we help
others assume the role of host as well?

A key image related to convening for many
is the circle. "We exercise our power in circles," the
leader of a grassroots movement told me, "which
is Eucharistic. Not in triangles." A cofounder of the
Leadership Roundtable described how the very name
of the organization evolved from the image of the circle.
"We chose the round table to be symbolic of how we
wanted to relate to all those seated at the table," she
noted. Like Rashi's interpretation of the "us" in Genesis
1:26, humility is valued. "Anyone who comes to one of
our convenings," she continued, "could be a keynoter
in their own right, but all have to check their egos at
the door and sit at the round table. We try to do lots of
breakout discussions to make sure as many people get
to talk with one another as possible and that it is not
just one person talking up front."

Leaders spoke about how they were trying
to be increasingly intentional about widening the
circle of voices invited to committees, meetings, and
conferences. They wanted to make these gatherings
accessible: using the closed-caption function on Zoom,
providing simultaneous translation, and seeking
scholarship funds for those who might have a hard
time paying conference fees.

Beyond getting people to the table, however, they
spoke about the importance of designing meetings
in such a way that all the voices present were heard
and everyone had the chance to share in "hosting"
functions. Often this meant assigning different

leadership roles in a gathering to different people: one person serving as the facilitator, another as the time monitor, and another as the group scribe. Roles could rotate from one gathering to the next. A couple of leaders I spoke to had sought out training in specific processes such as The Circle Way (thecircleway.net) or Sociocracy (sociocracyforall.org) to help them exercise their power of convening in healthier and holier ways. Both approaches make the image of the circle central to their design.

Interestingly, however, Christian leaders express the grief of sometimes feeling left out of circles themselves. Part of this might be due to the Martha dilemma: it is hard to both host a gathering and be fully present to enjoy it at the same time. When we are in the role of the convener, it can be difficult to simultaneously participate as a member of the conversation, especially if it involves a sticky topic that one has strong personal opinions about.

Part of the sadness, though, relates to a broader experience of no longer being able to participate in the same way within circles of support and friendship that one enjoyed before differences in power were magnified. Many leaders describe how being appointed to a new leadership role, having something they'd written go viral, or landing a major gig created challenges in existing relationships. Old friends, and even family members, began to treat them differently—taking occasional potshots, making snide comments, or asking for favors.

Sometimes their new positions gave them access to confidential information that could not be shared with those who used to be their peers. Often, they could no longer share their work dilemmas openly, or the nature of those dilemmas was not something others would be able to understand. The situation is particularly acute for those who are promoted within their own institutions, for example, someone who served on the faculty and becomes the principal or a principal who becomes superintendent within their own diocese or school board. "When I first got promoted to administration within the hospital," a former vice president for mission relayed, "I felt good about the promotion but lousy about what it did to my relationship with fellow chaplains. I wasn't one of them anymore. I lost my sense of affiliation."

As Christian leaders, we, too, need supportive, confidential spaces for sharing about dilemmas that are real in our lives. Leadership can be lonely, and we also need circles. "Never in a million years did I imagine I'd join Legatus,"[3] the CEO of a large nonprofit told me, "but it has become a lifeline. It's the only place people understand the types of issues I'm dealing with." Yet, as he readily acknowledged, circles of leaders run the danger of becoming the most exclusive kinds of circles there are. Even as he remains devoted to widening circles of belonging and access in his own offices, he knows he now has the personal cell phone numbers of ten other CEOs whom he can call, and they will answer—a privilege few have. Are such circles inherently triangles? Are there holy and healthy ways to live this kind of relational power as well?

The power of convening is at once one of the most fundamental and most complicated powers we experience as humans. With the surge of interest in and commitment to creating communities that are diverse, equitable, and inclusive, it is the power that is perhaps under the greatest scrutiny at present. As Christian leaders we, like Jesus, want to be open, as much as life allows, to gather with whoever asks us to join their table, realizing this practice may be critiqued: Why are you meeting with sinners? Or with Pharisees? Or with Democrats/Republicans? Take your pick. Sometimes we may have to maneuver ourselves into finding a seat at tables where we are not yet invited. Sometimes we may even have to overturn tables that perpetuate injustice. But as leaders, likely our most regular and most profound exercise of this power will be in how we take on the role of the convener—whom we call to the table, how we welcome, and how we host. All of the above are part of the way we act "in memory of him."

Companion for the Journey: **Samuel Mazzuchelli**

> There he is, high upon the scaffold of a church,
> with coat off and sleeves tucked up, industriously
> at work in brick and mortar. In the evening you see
> him in the pulpit discoursing on some abstruse
> question of Christian philosophy and tomorrow
> he lectures before . . . legislators on the science of
> political economy, but always and everywhere
> present when the sacred duties of the ministry are
> required. Wonderful little man![4]

These words, written by an Iowa judge about Fr.
Samuel Mazzuchelli, offer a window into the busy
life of this Italian missionary who dedicated his entire
ministry to convening and building up communities
across the Upper Midwest of the United States.
Where did he gain all this knowledge of architecture,
philosophy, and political science, not to mention
scripture, astronomy, and the ability to communicate in
at least six languages? That is only part of the mystery
of this "wonderful little man."

Mazzuchelli was born in 1806 to a large, influential
family in Milan filled with politicians, artists, bankers,
and scholars. But at the age of only seventeen, he left
the rich intellectual milieu of his home city to join
the struggling Dominican community in Faenza,
150 miles away. And though the Dominicans sent
him on for studies in Rome, while still a seminarian

Mazzuchelli sought permission to join the Dominican bishop Edward Fenwick in the newly created diocese of Cincinnati in the United States. His formal education ceased—but not his zeal for life and learning.

Fenwick was desperate for priests to serve in his far-flung diocese, which included not only all of Ohio but also Michigan and parts of Wisconsin. After mentoring Mazzuchelli for two years, Fenwick ordained him and assigned him as priest of the "Northwest Territories" with particular care for Mackinac Island, Green Bay, and Sault Ste. Marie. He was twenty-four years old, facing a bitterly cold environment he'd never encountered before. At the time, he knew little English and no indigenous languages. There was not another priest, never mind another Dominican, for hundreds of miles. But whereas others might have found the assignment daunting, the energetic and outgoing Mazzuchelli could not wait to go.

Mazzuchelli arrived to Mackinac in October 1830. The island had a tiny church but had never had a resident priest. Until he was able to build his own cottage, Mazzuchelli was offered shelter by Madeleine LaFramboise, granddaughter of the local Odawa chief and owner of a fur trading company. She introduced him to the bustling island community made up of Metis, Ojibwe, and French Canadians, making sure he would feel a sense of belonging. Using Mackinac as a home base, Mazzuchelli began to travel by foot, canoe, and horseback to meet the people of this vast territory. Many, like LaFramboise, already identified as Catholic but had not been able to participate in the sacraments for decades. Mazzuchelli gathered together the Catholics in each settlement, celebrating Eucharist, hearing their confessions, blessing their marriages, and baptizing their children. He helped them begin to think of themselves as local congregations and to raise funds for building their own churches.

The first church that Mazzuchelli constructed was St. John the Evangelist Church in Green Bay, Wisconsin, in 1831. In his book *The Memoirs of Father Samuel Mazzuchelli, OP*, he gives readers a detailed description of the building process on the frontier: "Imagine a stone foundation . . . rising about three feet above ground, with a length of eighty and a width of thirty-eight feet. Upon this wall are laid oak beams, one and one-fourth feet square, and from 30 to 40 feet long, firmly joined together. Into these beams, which are called joists, others of lighter weight are fitted, mortised, and fastened."[5] Clearly, this was a man with the mind of an architect, yet no one knows where he learned all of his building design skills.

Over the next thirty years, Mazzuchelli established thirty-five local parish communities in the Upper Midwest and erected twenty church buildings where these communities might gather, six of which still remain in use.[6] He not only designed and supervised the construction but also would often add extra touches of his own hand to beautify the interior, learning how to make wood look like marble or carving an ornate tabernacle. In addition, he assisted with the design of civic buildings, including the first Iowa State House, and mapped out the streets of the town of Shullsburg, Wisconsin.

After five years in the far north, Mazzuchelli's pastoring responsibilities shifted southwest to the "tri-state" area where the borders of Wisconsin, Illinois, and Iowa meet. At one point, he was the only priest along a two-hundred-mile stretch of the Mississippi River from Prairie du Chien, Wisconsin, to Rock Island, Illinois. He worked unceasingly to create a sense of "us" among Irish and German immigrants, many of whom were far from their families while working in the lead mines.

Mazzuchelli, though, did experience loneliness himself. As the only priest in the vicinity, he longed for a peer to talk with. For a short while, that need was met in Fr. Frederic Baraga—a Slovenian priest who came to work among the Odawa people forty miles south of Mackinac. On several occasions, Mazzuchelli made the trek to visit Baraga for confession and spiritual direction, including in the dead of winter when "the wondrous power of nature had at one stroke frozen the waters which separate the island . . . [and] prepared a dry road for the missionary." He continues, "Few persons can realize the emotion of two priests who, after months of solitude, have the consolation of meeting."[7]

Once settled in the tri-state area, Mazzuchelli tried desperately to convene a community of Dominican brothers with whom to share a common life, but he met an endless stream of challenges. In the end, his closest companions were the women he gathered to become Dominican sisters, later known as the Sinsinawa Dominicans.

Under Mazzuchelli's wing, these women, mostly from local Irish families, founded some of the first schools in the area, including the renowned St. Clara's Academy in Benton, Wisconsin. Mazzuchelli was immensely proud of this all-girls secondary school, making sure those who attended had access to a wide variety of musical instruments and the most advanced scientific instruments of the time. He was also immensely proud of the sisters, whom he admired for their joy and daring, so similar to his own. "What impressed me from the beginning regarding Fr. Samuel," commented a sister who came to join his community, "was his courtesy and consideration of [the sisters]."[8]

In January 1864, Mazzuchelli was greatly saddened by the sudden death of Sr. Clara Conway, one of the first women to have joined the Sinsinawa community and one of its strongest leaders. "When he stood in the little chapel looking at the bier beside the altar, he hesitated in deep emotion three times before he could begin Mass," a sister observed.[9] He had lost one of those rare, treasured peers in ministry.

Only a few weeks later, Mazzuchelli—known for never getting sick—took ill with pneumonia after making two house calls on an abysmally cold night. He died on February 23 reciting Psalm 84, the prayer offered at the dedication of every newly constructed church: "How lovely is your dwelling place, O Lord!" Having convened so many communities and built so many churches, Mazzuchelli had gone to join the house of the Lord in the community of saints.

For Reflection

- How do you see Jesus trying to build a sense of "us" throughout his ministry?

- What tables have you been invited to because of your leadership? How do you decide which ones to join? Are there tables you won't sit at out of principle? Why?

- Do you have a sense of people "coming when you call"? Have you ever attributed this to power before?

- What have you tried of late to widen the diversity of people you call to the table? Have you experimented with ways of sharing the hosting role by rotating leadership of gatherings or creating a variety of roles? What have you discovered?

- What circles of support do you have in your life as a leader? Are there circles where you no longer feel welcome?

- What do you glean from the life of Fr. Samuel Mazzuchelli about what it means to live power in a healthy and holy way, particularly as it relates to calling people together?

5. Exercising the Power to Bless

God blessed them, saying: Be fertile,
multiply, and fill the water of the seas; and
let the birds multiply on the earth.

—Genesis 1:22

God blessed them and God said to them:
Be fertile and multiply; fill the earth and
subdue it. Have dominion over the fish of
the sea, the birds of the air, and all the living
things that crawl on the earth.

—Genesis 1:28

The opening verses of Genesis describe something wild
and crazy. Yes, creation is a well-organized endeavor;
everything emerges in an orderly fashion. We talked
about that in chapter 3. But look again more closely
and you'll discover that ordered is not the same as
tame. When God brings forth life, it teems or, in other
translations, swarms.[1] It is abundant, overflowing,
and a bit out of control. And then God does something
that might seem insane. God looks at what is already
teeming and swarming and chooses to share the power

of fertility, so that what is teeming and swarming might not only replicate but also exponentially *increase*—often translated as "multiply." It happens through a blessing.

Blessing first appears in the Bible in Genesis 1:22. God blesses (*way-barek*) the creatures of the sea and sky. But it is certainly not the last time there is a blessing. It happens a few verses later in Genesis 1:28 when God blesses humans in a similar way. And the word *barek* or some derivative of it will reappear approximately five hundred times more in the pages to come. Sometimes humans will bless God. Sometimes humans will bless other humans. But often, as here, God does the blessing. What ties all of these different blessings together is that they always involve a scene in which power is shared as a gift. In Hebrew, the root word for blessing is the word for "knee," which may seem odd, but in blessing there is a bending of the knee toward the other, an honoring of the other. The giver blesses by the passing on of a treasured power. The recipient blesses by verbalizing gratitude for the gift and then using it—not letting the gift sit but making the most of it.

It might seem that the scariest part of blessing from the perspective of the giver lies in letting go of some of one's power. So often we think of power akin to a bank account. Being generous with power is considered a noble thing, but one must watch the bottom line. If I share my power with you, I have less, and no one wants to go into the red. But from a Genesis perspective, remember that power is abundant. God is the mint. There is always more where that came from. To use another metaphor, power is like a flame. The lighting of one candle from another never diminishes the original light. It only makes for more light.

From a Genesis perspective, the scariest part of giving a blessing is not that we might run out of power but rather that once a blessing is given it cannot be taken back. One cannot control how the light will spread— whether it will illumine or blind, warm or burn. Take the blessing of fertility in Genesis 1. We might desire a world in which life's teeming and swarming is well regulated so that it leads only to outcomes that please us, but this is not how blessing works, especially when we are thinking in terms of exponential multiplication. The same evolutionary process that has led over time to an exquisite array of colorful parrots and sweet-smelling orchids and more pepper varieties than we can count has also led to mosquitos and mutating viruses and cancer cells.

Scripture scholar Gerhard Lohfink suggests that God understood this would be the case and still chose the path of blessing. God could have fashioned "a complete, sterile, glass house of a world, a lotusland in which happiness is prefabricated," Lohfink states. "[But] in such a world there would be no freedom and therefore, no real love. In such a world we would be mere marionettes."[2] When God chooses to bless creation—including humans—with the power of fertility, God elects for "a world in which there is love, which comes from freedom; in which there is suffering that allows people to mature; in which there is misfortune that tests them . . . a world that is not yet finished, a world where humans can join in."[3]

Jesus was one who embraced and modeled the path of blessing, with all of its joys and risks. Luke chapters 9 and 10 offer a fascinating window into his commitment to this path. In chapter 9 he calls together the Twelve to involve them in that world that is not yet finished: the coming reign of God. He sends them out to preach the Good News just as he has been sent by God and to share in his ministry. They are to go without money or possessions, but before they depart, Jesus shares with them the power he has been given to heal illness and to subject demons so that the Twelve might not only speak about the reign of God but also give illustration to what it is all about, just as Jesus himself does.

Later in the chapter, the Twelve complain to Jesus that they've encountered another who is casting out demons in Jesus's name but who is not one of their number. Jesus is not threatened by this news in the least. His attitude seems to be "the more the merrier." "Whoever is not against you is for you," he says (Lk 9:50). A few verses later at the start of chapter 10, Jesus sends out not twelve but seventy-two disciples, multiplying the ministry sixfold. When the seventy-two return thrilled that—yes—they *have* been able to subject demons, he is equally thrilled and turns to praise God from whom all blessings flow. The fact that Jesus's disciples are also successful does not make him jealous or possessive. It is his joy.

Even for Jesus, though, not every act of shared power continues in the trajectory Jesus would have hoped. The gospels make clear that Jesus's disciples were not always effective in their healing efforts. In the middle of Luke chapter 9, there is a boy with a demon they couldn't cast out. Their power seems to have fizzled rather than multiplied. Moreover, the disciples did not entirely understand the reign of God, even as they were sent to preach about it. They still expect Jesus to ascend in the power structures of the day, acquiring wealth and political dominance, and they want to be right beside him as he does so. A few verses after the failed healing in chapter 9, Jesus finds his disciples in an argument with each other about who is "greatest." Their hopes for earthly power versus reign-of-God power crystalize in the person of Judas whose eventual betrayal of Jesus brings to mind the warning from Machiavelli: "He who is the cause of another becoming powerful is ruined."[4] Yes, that is always a danger.

It is the unknown and uncontrollable outcomes that make blessing difficult for us to embrace as Christian leaders. Leaders are often critiqued for overmanaging, nagging, and not being willing to "let go" and "share power." The challenge is that many who have tried to "let go" and trust others to "run with it" have at some point in their lives felt burned. Although probably not to the degree that Judas violated Jesus's trust, many of us have felt the pain of betrayal. I spoke with a school principal whose board had challenged her again and again to delegate more. "I try. I try so hard," she said.

> Last summer I passed on to a staff member the research and writing of a grant that was supposed to be relatively easy to get and would make a huge difference in our school. Whenever I asked how it was going, he told me the writing was well underway. He was making good progress. I trusted. Then on the day the grant needed to be submitted, I saw he'd filled out the wrong forms and cut and pasted a bunch of stuff from a previous grant that wasn't applicable to this one. Aaagh. I spent all afternoon frantically rewriting the grant. We didn't get it. Did I let go too much here? . . . Probably.

And therein lies the dilemma. We want to trust, share, delegate, and bless. We want to give people the freedom to be creative and even the freedom to make mistakes. At the same time, many of us try to live by the motto "The buck stops here." We ourselves are often answerable to supervisors or boards and need to take responsibility for the ultimate results of the actions of those who report to us. We worry our own livelihoods may be endangered by the actions of others, and more so, we worry that the organizations or ministries we care about could be endangered. The principal's school *really* would have benefited from that grant.

"I love using my power to empower," a director of school accreditation told me. "I want to give schools a lot of freedom in how they might creatively meet the standards." The founder of a Christian online movement told me how, in the last year, she entirely revamped her popular website to include a wide diversity of authors, not only her own writing. "It is so great to feature people who haven't been published before. It is so great to share the mic," she said. Yet both admitted that it remains scary. Not all schools are up to the challenge, and the quality of students' learning experiences could be compromised. Not all authors elicit the same number of "likes," and it is her own family's income that is on the line if the new website fails.

For many leaders, the healthy middle road between complete trust in the creative juices of others and a tightisted control of every process going forward involves mentorship appropriate to the coworker's readiness. In his book *Multiply the Ministry*, longtime ministry consultant Sean Reynolds describes four stages each of us moves through if we remain in the work long enough:

- Beginner: the stage in which we don't know all that we don't know and hence are prone to make serious blunders

- Apprentice: the stage in which we know that we don't know everything and so are inclined to be nervous and seek out advice

- Partner: the stage in which we know what we know and want to be trusted for our expertise

- Master: the stage in which we don't know all that we know and hence can get frustrated that others lack what we consider to be common sense[5]

When supervising someone who is a beginner or apprentice, setting the person free to be creative in whatever way they see fit without any guidance could be viewed as noble, but it could also be viewed as irresponsible—both for the good of the ministry and for the good of the supervisee who may experience the freedom as flailing or lack of support.

Genesis is a story of blessing, but it is not a story of abandonment. The God who blesses also remains alongside the blessed—something we will talk about more in chapter 10. It makes sense as a supervisor to ask for updates, set up regular check-ins, and not wait until there is a problem. If managing someone who has proven to be a partner though, it makes sense to give a lot of trust and autonomy. Anything less will feel restricting and demeaning. Wait to give advice until asked for it.

The greatest managerial challenge, of course, is the period of transition between apprentice and partner. Here is where we as supervisors will likely encounter friction, either because we think the other is ready to be on their own, yet they are still wanting our presence and support, or because the other believes they should be given more freedom and we still see the need for mentorship.

When someone we supervise becomes a master in their own right, it is important that they themselves become involved in mentoring in order not to stagnate. Every master in their field needs to be reminded of what it is like to be a beginner again and see things with fresh eyes. Indeed, if one reaches the stage of master and does not share power with others, the office becomes a fiefdom. It is irresponsible for the good of the ministry not to consider succession planning.

The board member of a family philanthropic foundation described to me her journey through these four stages:

> Before they died, my great-grandparents decided they wanted all of their resources to be dedicated to funding projects in the Church. They also decided that their children and grandchildren would be charged with stewarding these resources and would never be paid themselves for this work. We can begin to serve within the foundation as soon as we become teenagers, and this has gone on now for five generations. We have a special commitment to attend to the youngest members of the foundation. It is terrifying when you are fourteen to be sent out for the first time to represent

the family or to be asked for your opinion during a committee meeting. But you soon realize the family has your back and wants you to gain this experience. Serving in this foundation has been the most incredible privilege. It has been a blessing.

Indeed, this service was a "blessing" for her in the most ancient biblical sense of the word.

The fact that Jesus's sharing of power with his disciples did not always lead to desirable results—indeed contributed to his own death—did not stop Jesus from continuing to share his power with them. The Gospel of Luke ends with Jesus blessing his disciples. Soon they will be sent out again to preach the reign of God in every nook and cranny of the planet. The earth is to teem and swarm with good news. But Jesus promises that they will not go out to multiply the ministry on their own. They are commanded to first wait in Jerusalem until they are "clothed with power from on high" (Lk 24:49). The disciples will now have with them the same Spirit that animated Jesus's life, and they will be mentored every next step of the way according to their need.

Companion for the Journey:
Jean-Baptiste de La Salle

We often speak of choices that lead one down a slippery slope toward greater and greater evil, but rarely do we consider there are also choices casually made that lead one careening recklessly toward greater and greater good. Jean-Baptiste de La Salle described such a choice in his own life shortly before he died: "Indeed, if I had ever thought that the care I was taking of the schoolmasters out of pure charity would have made it my duty to live with them, I would have dropped the whole project."[6] Fortunately for the rest of us, he had no idea what he was getting himself into.

The schoolmasters de La Salle referenced were a rowdy bunch. A contemporary described them as "gamblers, drunkards, libertines, ignorant, brutal, card-players in taverns, fiddlers in haunts of pleasure."[7] They had been hired by a zealous do-gooder Adrien Nyel to help launch a school for impoverished boys in Reims, France, but frankly the teachers were in as much need of help as the students.

At the time he met Nyel, de La Salle was a newly ordained priest from a prestigious family in town. He was a board member at the city's university and canon in the Reims Cathedral, one of the elite inner circle who advised the archbishop, with a salary set for life. In addition, de La Salle had his hands full caring for his family's estate and the education of his younger siblings after the death of his parents. His life was busy, and his future was bright . . . but then there were these teachers.

De La Salle admired Nyel. He knew the need for charity schools was great. France in the second half of the seventeenth century was a highly stratified society. Rich families like de La Salle's provided their children with private tutors. But working-class families might at best give their children two or three years of remedial Latin in a "little school," and many could not afford even that. Nyel's commitment to open free schools for poor families was noble, but in his passion for the cause, he had launched more schools than he could reasonably manage. The inexperienced teachers were flailing. And so de La Salle stepped in to help with quality control in the personnel department.

He rented a house for Nyel's teachers so they could have a steady diet and lodging. He began to offer them lessons in how to not only teach but also be models for the students. And then at the nudge of his spiritual director, in 1631, he invited the teachers to move in with him at his family's estate. "In fact, I experienced a great deal of unpleasantness when I first had them come to my house," he admitted. "This lasted for two years."[8] His siblings were so upset by his choice that they forced him to sell the house, requiring him to rent a place for the budding community nearby. But under de La Salle's mentorship, the schoolmasters were developing into fine educators, and the classrooms they served were not just multiplying but thriving. Requests to staff more schools poured in. Where to go first? How not to spread themselves too thin as Nyel had done?

De La Salle urged the teachers to trust providence, but they replied that as a canon from a wealthy family, this was far easier for him than for them. De La Salle considered their words and then made two even more radical decisions. He decided to leave his role as canon and the income associated with it and to give away all of his inherited wealth to those suffering from famine. Between 1683 and 1684, de La Salle distributed what today would be the equivalent of five hundred thousand dollars, leaving himself as vulnerable as the schoolmasters themselves. Those who remained with him in the aftermath of these choices took the name "Brothers of the Christian Schools."

De La Salle not only let go of the prestige and wealth of his upbringing but also demanded that—although ordained as a priest—he be treated as a brother. He insisted the brothers elect one of their own as leader and that he be as obedient to whoever was elected as the rest. Although this did not go over well with the bishop, de La Salle fought his whole life to share power with the brothers and to protect their internal governance from any sort of interference by pastors or donors. The commitment won him few friends among Church leaders and even sometimes irked his brothers.

At multiple points over the next three decades, de La Salle might easily have rued the day he crossed paths with Nyel. The size of the Christian Brothers community waxed and waned as new brothers came, but now experienced brothers often found more lucrative teaching opportunities elsewhere and left the community. De La Salle became tangled in an expensive lawsuit with a wealthy donor's family. At times, he probably wished he had back some of the power he had given away to be able to influence situations more positively. But by this point, de La Salle was already too far down his chosen path of blessing to turn around. "God did this in an imperceptible way and over a long period of time," he said, "so that one commitment led to another in a way that I did not foresee in the beginning."[9]

The years 1711–1714 were particularly hard ones for de La Salle as he retreated from the hub of his community's life in Paris to visit brothers in the south of France and pray for clarity about what to do next. He wanted to step away from any leadership role among the brothers whatsoever and contemplated becoming the sacramental minister at a rural retreat house called Parmenie. But the woman who ran the retreat center— although in desperate need of a resident priest— counseled him, "In no way should you abandon the family God has given you. . . . You must persevere in it even unto death."[10]

Shortly thereafter, de La Salle received a letter from his brothers in Paris commanding him under obedience to return and help stabilize the community. The brothers were taking seriously the power he had been trying to entrust to them! Humbly, de La Salle returned, stating, "Well, I am here, what do you want of me?" For the remaining five years of his life, de La Salle mentored Br. Barthélemy as he stepped into his role as the first formally elected lay leader of the Christian Brothers.

De La Salle was the community's last priest but the first of its many brothers. Presently, the Lasallian Christian Brothers are found in eighty countries and sponsor approximately 1,100 educational institutions. In the spirit of de La Salle, the three thousand brothers continue to share their power and magnify their impact by collaborating with a vast network of ninety thousand Lasallian lay coworkers, serving an estimated one million students globally.[11]

For Reflection

- How do you understand Gerhard Lohfink's assertion that a world that had no mosquitos or viruses would also be a world incapable of love?

- What are your experiences of trying to share power with others? Do you have both positive and negative experiences? What determines this?

- When considering your current leadership role, where do you see yourself in Sean Reynolds's ministry arc (beginner, apprentice, partner, or master)?

- Have you received mentoring in your own life? What did you value about the experience? Have you ever mentored someone? What was that like?

- What do you glean from the story of Jean-Baptiste de La Salle's life that adds to your understanding of a spirituality of power, especially the commitment to share power through blessing?

6. Exercising the Power to Draw Boundaries

The Lord God took the man and settled him in the garden of Eden, to cultivate and care for it. The Lord God gave the man this order: You are free to eat from any of the trees of the garden except the tree of knowledge of good and evil. From that tree you shall not eat; when you eat from it you shall die.

—Genesis 2:15–17

Why not eat from that tree? Isn't knowledge a good thing? Why wouldn't God want us to have knowledge? Why set this tree apart from the rest?

Boundaries are often quite difficult to understand. They raise questions. They can seem unfair or arbitrary. Sometimes they are the source of sadness and grief. Our Jewish ancestors in the faith recognized this. They also recognized that boundaries serve a purpose. They are necessary for life to flourish.

The fundamental importance of boundaries is established in the opening verses of the first story of creation in which God creates (*bara*) by separating:

setting light apart from dark, setting the water below apart from the water above, and setting land apart from the sea. Each has its own space. The word *bara* actually comes from the Hebrew root word meaning "to slash, to chop." Something that was one has now been cleaved into two, each to keep within its own confines.

Jewish midrash claims that when the waters below were separated from the waters above, they wept. A close reading of the Genesis text reveals that the day this separation of the waters took place—the second day of creation—is the only one that ends without God declaring it "good." Jewish commentator Avivah Zornberg notes, "*Havdalah*—separation, specialization, the formation of difference and opposition—is generally achieved at some sacrifice."[1] And yet none of us would exist if this *havdalah* had not taken place. The boundaries between light and dark, sky and sea, and sea and land are what have enabled each space to develop on its own and serve different elements of creation that cannot coexist in the same space (e.g., fish and birds) yet are necessary for the whole to flourish.

In the second story of creation, we are asked to trust the same is true—that God has a good reason for setting the Tree of Knowledge of Good and Evil apart from the other trees—but it is even harder to accept. God says that this boundary, too, is necessary for life as eating from the tree will result in death. But in this case, it raises doubts: Will we really die? Is there another reason God isn't saying? Something God doesn't want us to have? The fruit of the tree is so desirable. Perhaps God is greedy, unwilling to share? And, really, why wouldn't God want us to have knowledge?

An entire wing of a library could be dedicated solely to books written about the Tree of Knowledge of Good and Evil and the boundary encircling it. Within Christian tradition, God's boundary around the tree is often conceived of as a test: God wants to see whether the humans will obey God's command simply because God gave it. They don't need to understand why. The catastrophic events that follow are viewed as divine punishment for being disobedient. Within Judaism— where having a feisty, argumentative relationship with God is treasured rather than discouraged—the boundary is more often understood as it is in the first story of creation: meant to offer a necessary protective barrier, even if only for a time.

Jewish commentators—and, interestingly, early Christian commentators like Irenaeus—tend to think of the "Adam and Eve" characters in the text not as adults but children, who someday may be ready for "knowledge of good and evil" but not yet. The thirteenth-century rabbi Nachmanides, for example, asserted that human beings, as creatures of the earth, were always going to be mortal but that God thought the weight of this knowledge would crush them. Nachmanides interpreted Genesis 2:17 to mean not that the man and woman would immediately die but that they would immediately know that they would die. God established the boundary around the tree as a kindness, so that the man and woman would be protected from a burdensome knowledge no other creature has to bear.[2]

Other Jewish commentators have understood the tree as representing sexual awareness. The Hebrew word for "knowledge" used here—*da'at*—often refers to intimate or sexual knowledge.[3] They note that it is only *after* eating of the tree that the man and woman realize they are naked and that the woman receives the name Eve (*Chavvah*), meaning "first mother." Again, perhaps it is not that humans were *never* meant to have this kind of knowledge but rather that—fresh from the earth—they were not ready yet. From a Jewish perspective, the events that follow describe a waking up to adult existence. The experience of work as toil, pain in childbearing, and awareness of death are not divine punishment; they are the natural consequences of stepping over the boundary into adulthood.

Much of the current literature on boundaries underscores their protective intention: Good boundaries exist to keep things that cannot coexist in the same space separate from one another so that different kinds of life may flourish on their own and, in doing so, serve the greater good of the whole. Good boundaries protect others. They protect us. And they protect the causes and communities we seek to serve.

If we consider, in particular, boundaries in the workplace, we might think first of boundaries related to physical safety. We realize no one should have to work in an environment that might make them sick or lead to injury and that people need to work in spaces that are free from intimidation and threat of bodily violence.

Closely related, sexual boundaries have long been of paramount concern. Cultures around the world differ greatly in terms of what kinds of boundaries feel important to establish in this regard between men and women, and children and adults, but all cultures have them because sexuality deals with the mystery of life itself continuing. If we want our species to continue, of course we will care about boundaries that protect bodily integrity and sexual expression. In fact, the very first code of professional ethics known in human history—the Hippocratic Oath for physicians written around 500 BC—draws special attention to sexual boundaries: "Whatever house I may visit, I will come for the benefit of the sick, remaining free of all intentional injustice, of all mischief, and in particular of sexual relations with both female and male persons, be they free or slaves."[4] Twenty-five hundred years later, we could say we are still trying to make sure no one is touched in ways that are uncomfortable or troubling to them and that no one is exposed to information or visuals they are not ready for. We certainly do not want anyone to be pressured or forced into a relationship they don't want to have.

Beyond boundaries serving physical and sexual safety, however, much has been written of late on the importance of boundaries related to psychological safety in the workplace. We want to support the development of healthy minds and spirits by creating environments that are free of derogatory humor, ethnic and racial slurs, gender stereotyping, and persistent political messaging. We desire clarity on behavioral expectations related to our professions—both inside the work environment and outside that environment, for example, on social media. A subcategory of boundaries supporting psychological safety is boundaries concerning workload and time spent on the job. We want clarity about where one staff member's responsibilities begin and another's end, and we need to watch that workload is distributed in a balanced way. We need norms on when to be checking emails and when we are "off the clock" so that work doesn't overflow into every aspect of our lives.

Drawing boundaries—physical, sexual, and psychological—is a task every human is about from infancy. We begin to develop boundaries the day we realize as infants that our mothers' bodies are not our own, that there is a separation between us and yet a relationship that remains. Throughout childhood and adolescence, indeed well into adulthood, we are constantly learning through experience where to draw the lines that assert our independence—again, not so we can cut ourselves off from others but so we can be ever more interdependent with more people in healthy ways.

With leadership, however, comes heightened responsibility for drawing and maintaining boundaries. Why? This is because, as named earlier, leaders enjoy not only "power to" but also "power over." Those who experience less power in any relationship are more vulnerable to having their boundaries crossed. In the workplace, for example, they are more likely to be asked to work late without the freedom to say no. They are more likely to be touched in ways that make them feel uncomfortable. They are more likely to have jobs that place them in physical danger or on the front lines.

In contrast, those with more power in any relationship are more likely to cross others' boundaries without knowing they've done so. They are more likely to initiate physical contact that another did not ask for. They are more likely to request favors, name expectations, or assign workloads that others will have a hard time resisting. The weight of responsibility for naming and maintaining good boundaries tilts in our direction as leaders because we are more likely to be the ones who will need boundaries to keep from doing others harm.

The responsibility for drawing and maintaining boundaries as a leader, however, does not end with tending to one's own boundaries. Leaders by definition have a community of persons looking to them and bear heightened responsibility for tending to life in the community as a whole. Alas, this task sounds more straightforward than it actually is. While everyone seems to agree that boundaries such as national borders are a good idea, often people disagree about where exactly they should be. As such, boundaries, as with national borders, are frequently places of tension where power is most visibly at play in the life of the the community.

One of the things that makes establishing and maintaining boundaries tough at a communal level is that our individual senses of where good boundaries lie are highly shaped by our families of origin, cultures, generations, and religious upbringings. In leading a community, one is often negotiating among many different persons' individual boundaries. Is establishing a dress code in the workplace a way of protecting the dignity of the human body, or is it body shaming and associating the body with vice? Is setting an organization-wide practice of "no email over the weekend" a necessary protection for people's family lives or an assault on their autonomy: why is it your business when I choose to work?

When we set boundaries within an organization that are unaligned with others' expectations, just as in the case of Adam and Eve, our motives are often viewed with suspicion: Why do you get to make this call? Shouldn't I be able to decide what's best for me here? Who are you to decide what is "inappropriate"? In others' eyes, either you are caving in to political correctness or you are being insensitive to legitimate concerns. You are being unfair or you are being arbitrary. You must have another reason you just aren't saying. You want to keep the tree all for yourself. In every organization, it isn't that people "don't have boundaries." It's more likely they all have them but are drawing them in different places and having a hard time agreeing on where they should be.

Leadership in the Christian community adds a further layer of complication in that many Christian communities have a history of lifting up Jesus as someone who broke boundaries and who tore down walls of separation. Shouldn't we do likewise? We look to his example on the Cross and say, "Love has no boundaries." Shouldn't he be the model for our organizations? We hear his words about forgiving seventy times seven and think that we need to let those who "trespass against us"—an image of boundary violation—continue to be given yet another opportunity to do so. How do we as Christian leaders establish and maintain healthy boundaries within our ministries when Christian scripture, at least at face value, appears so dismissive of them?

The witness of Jesus does offer an important nuance to the Genesis perspective on boundaries that we've not yet mentioned: boundaries are important and are meant to serve life, but from daily life, we know that not all boundaries do so. There are nonnegotiable—sometimes called *intrinsic*—boundaries that are woven into the fabric of existence on planet Earth. For example, if I cross the boundary between myself and the fireplace, I will get burned.

Intrinsic boundaries have their own natural, generally immediate, consequences. Yet often the consequences of violating an intrinsic boundary are so severe that we will draw an outer ring around the intrinsic boundary that we might call an "imposed boundary."[5] For example, we place a grate eighteen inches in front of the fireplace. We give stern instructions to our children to stand back from the grate.

Over time, however, it turns out we humans have imposed many boundaries that were meant to protect not life but rather wealth, status quo, racial segregation, or other forms of power differential. Not all boundaries are good. It is possible that some boundaries are also bad. And it is true that Jesus did regularly test imposed boundaries and ask questions about who the boundaries were really protecting. He frequently challenged the pharisaical interpretation of the law as unnecessarily burdensome and divisive within the community.

In imitation of Jesus, we, too, should raise questions when it is unclear what good a boundary is serving and whose well-being is being protected.

Furthermore, we should be open to *being questioned* about the boundaries we've imposed as leaders, be able to articulate our rationale, and be prepared to redraw the boundary if there is a greater good for the "less powerful" members of the community pointed out to us.

Jesus's life and teaching also inject important questions into contemporary discourse that views interpersonal boundaries as self-evident and inflexible and is quick to label relationships where there are boundary disagreements as "toxic." There are certainly relationships that are poisonous for everyone involved. (I have been in a few myself.) At the same time, our society's current conversation about boundaries tends to lack curiosity about how different cultures and generations may have come to define their norms under very different circumstances.

Jesus, especially in his teaching of the Lord's Prayer, seems to have anticipated that if we are living and working in close relationship with others, we are going to regularly step on each other's toes. We are each going to have expectations of each other that won't be met. Others are going to say things that hurt us and hold opinions we find offensive. Much as we try, we are not going to be able to create a world that is entirely free of friction simply by building good fences. Forgiveness of "trespasses" is not an occasion from Jesus's perspective but a way of being in the world. We will need to pray for help in this regard every day.

Yet, as Christian leaders, we need to also acknowledge how specific teachings and events in Jesus's life could be problematic if considered in isolation, outside the wider context of his life as a whole. There is a danger that we could hear Jesus's teaching on "turn the other cheek" and continue to put ourselves in situations where we become a punching bag. Worse, we may ask others to put themselves in such situations and to become accepting of abuse.

Love may have no boundaries, but boundaries are precisely what help us to know what true love looks like when put into action. Truly loving behavior does not allow bad behavior to go unchallenged. It does not rescue people from the natural consequences of their actions. It forgives, but it doesn't necessarily enter into circumstances where the same behavior could happen again. Truly loving behavior models the kind of boundary setting the other could emulate in order to flourish in life.

And if we look more widely at the gospels, we will see that Jesus did love in such a way. Jesus made personal sacrifices for others, but he also told people no. He would not work the miracle Herod wanted him to do. He would not answer Pilate's questions. He forgave, but he also held the Pharisees and Sadducees accountable for the impact of their teachings. He was active in ministry, but he also took time away by himself and had dinners with friends. He did not impose healing on people before checking in with them. "What do you want me to do for you?" he asked Bartimaeus on the road to Jericho (Mk 10:51). Jesus's boundless love was regularly expressed by honoring his own and others' boundaries.

And so, once again, in our exercise of Christian leadership, we find ourselves seeking a healthy and holy middle ground. Drawing on the ancient wisdom of scripture, we acknowledge the importance of good boundaries while, drawing on the same scriptures, acknowledging not all boundaries are good or the definitive solution to our interpersonal conflicts. We want to shape environments where people feel physically, sexually, and psychologically safe while acknowledging that each individual's sense of safety is highly personal and ultimately outside our sole capacity to meet. In short, we do the best we can. "One of the things I've come to realize," a school principal told me,

> is that every day requires something slightly different from me. Sometimes me being merciful with a particular family that has trespassed every boundary is a way I can help bring about greater justice in society as a whole, and sometimes me being just and drawing a strong boundary with a student is the greatest mercy I could do for them and their future. I'm always struggling to get it right.

We all are.

Companion for the Journey: **Kaloli Lwanga**

Kaloli—also known as Charles—Lwanga was born in 1860 in the burgeoning kingdom of Buganda, the southern region of what is now the country of Uganda. At the time of his birth, the kingdom was home to around two million people.[6] The walled palace compound in the capital city of Kampala was three miles in circumference. The kabaka, or king, was protected by an army of three thousand and served by five hundred young court attendants, many destined to become Buganda's future chiefs.

But Buganda's days as a powerful, independent kingdom were numbered. Arab traders were already making inroads within the kingdom, introducing Islam to the region. And when Lwanga was only two years old, the first European explorers arrived seeking the headwaters of the Nile. Shortly thereafter, both Catholic and Protestant missionaries arrived, alongside European entrepreneurs seeking access to Africa's bountiful natural resources. Efforts to colonize the continent soon followed, and for the next century, it became impossible to disentangle the religious, economic, and political motives behind Europe's presence in Africa.

As a young teen with leadership potential, Lwanga left his home along the shores of Lake Victoria to serve as an attendant in the court of Muteesa—one of the most prominent kabakas in Bugandan history. Muteesa was well aware of the Arab and European efforts to influence his kingdom and allowed Muslim, Protestant, and Catholic missionaries to all have a presence in his compound, often playing them against one another so that no one group became too influential. It was here in Muteesa's court that Lwanga was first introduced to Christianity by French missionaries and African lay catechists, including the leader of the royal attendants, Joseph Mukasa Balikuddembe.

When Muteesa died in 1884, Balikuddembe remained the majordomo for Muteesa's successor, his seventeen-year-old son Mwanga. The relationship, however, was never an easy one. Mwanga had a far more mercurial temperament than his father. He also led in an increasingly stressful time. The early months of his rule were marked by an outbreak of smallpox and severe drought. The German Imperial Army was laying claim to territory just to the south of Buganda. The British presence in his own region was becoming more pronounced by the day. Mwanga suspected that not only the missionaries but also the attendants they catechized were functioning as spies within his court. Mwanga expelled the missionaries and, in January 1885, ordered the arrest of all Bagandan men working for foreigners. Understandably, like any national leader, he wanted to protect the boundaries of his kingdom.

At the same time, Lwanga and Balikuddembe were renegotiating their own boundaries. It had been a norm in the court up to this point that attendants owed the kabaka absolute obedience, including sexual obedience. In their study of Christianity, however, they began to rethink what was owed the kabaka. They began to thwart Mwanga's sexual access to young attendants. Balikuddembe and Lwanga understood the kabaka's behavior to be a violation of the attendants' human dignity. Mwanga saw the situation as further evidence that European cultural norms were usurping his own.

Tensions came to a head in October 1885 when Mwanga ordered the execution of an Anglican bishop named James Hannington who had crossed into the kingdom of Buganda unannounced from the east, rather than via the normal southern road. While Hannington likely had no idea he had done something culturally offensive, for Mwanga, Hannington's behavior was akin to that of a robber sneaking in the backdoor instead of knocking on the front. When Balikuddembe argued for clemency and forgiveness of this boundary violation, it only reconfirmed Mwanga's conviction that he had traitors in his court. Not long after Hannington's death, Balikuddembe was also beheaded.

On the day of his mentor's death, Lwanga sought to be baptized and took over the role of majordomo. He continued his efforts to draw a boundary around the younger attendants, protecting them from the kabaka's sexual advances, and he continued to catechize within the court. He baptized many of the attendants himself. In May 1886, Mwanga called together all of the attendants and demanded that they renounce their Christian faith if they were truly loyal to the kabaka. As a group, the attendants refused, and Mwanga condemned them to death. They were chained together at the neck and forced to march for ten miles to Namugongo where they were imprisoned. On June 3, 1886, Kaloli Lwanga, twelve fellow Catholic attendants, and nine Anglican attendants were all burned to death. Lwanga, as the leader of the royal attendants, was separated from the rest to suffer in a particularly slow manner. He died shouting out, "Katonda!" (My God!).

There is probably much about Lwanga's story that we find uncomfortable: the intertwined nature of colonization and evangelization, the relationship between sex and power, the tension between one's culture and one's Christian faith, and the perils of cultural misunderstanding and different ways of interpreting the same events. Again, it is not that the persons involved lacked a sense of boundaries but that they were all seeing different boundaries as the boundaries that mattered most. Perhaps the reason we find the story *so* uncomfortable is that many of these tensions are still alive in our own time. It is no idyllic and simple world in which we are called to exercise Christian leadership, and yet like Lwanga, we know there are times when conscience will compel us to draw a line to protect those with less power from harm, regardless of the resistance we meet or the consequences we will endure.

For Reflection

- What are some examples of boundaries in your own life experience that you recognize have served the flourishing of life, such as the boundaries in the first creation story of Genesis? And what are examples of those that have not? How can you tell a difference between the two?

- What do you make of the notion that those with power are more responsible for tending to boundaries because they are the ones more likely to cross boundaries?

- What guidelines have you established for yourself as a leader about when to set and uphold a boundary? Are there any boundaries you've had to tweak over time?

- How does Jesus's teaching and witness on boundaries affirm or challenge your own sense of appropriate boundaries in the modern workplace?

- What insight do you glean from Kaloli Lwanga's story concerning the spirituality of power, especially as it relates to upholding healthy boundaries?

7. Exercising the Power to Remain Firm

Now the snake was the most cunning of all the wild animals that the LORD God had made. He asked the woman, "Did God really say, 'You shall not eat from any of the trees in the garden'?" The woman answered the snake: "We may eat of the fruit of the trees in the garden; it is only about the fruit of the tree in the middle of the garden that God said, 'You shall not eat it or even touch it, or else you will die.'" But the snake said to the woman: "You certainly will not die! God knows well that when you eat of it your eyes will be opened and you will be like gods, who know good and evil." The woman saw that the tree was good for food and pleasing to the eyes, and the tree was desirable for gaining wisdom. So she took some of its fruit and ate it; and she also gave some to her husband, who was with her, and he ate it.

—Genesis 3:1–6

Midway through this book, we are going to take a slight detour for a couple of pages. We have been talking about power as the capacity to *do* something, to change the environment. Power is the ability to make something happen, even if others wish it wouldn't. There is, however, a seemingly contradictory definition of power that I've not yet mentioned: power can also be understood as the ability to *resist* something happening, even when others wish that it would happen. Just as power is manifest in action, power is also manifest in inaction or remaining firm.

Throughout the Hebrew Scriptures, God is portrayed as possessing this capacity to remain unmoved. God is regularly described as faithful, steadfast, and true. No matter what is going on in the world beyond, God's word is unchanging, is trustworthy, and stands the test of time. In contrast, the people of God are portrayed as fickle, swaying like grass in the breeze. Their inability to withstand even the slightest temptation is captured well in the characters of Eve and Adam in the second story of creation.

Recall that this story was written down many centuries after Israel had entered into covenant relationship with God, many years after God had rescued the people from slavery in Egypt and wooed them out into the desert, and many years after they had received the gift of a law to live by as a sign of their unique relationship with God. Recall that Israel violated this law almost immediately after receiving it by fashioning an idol, and then violated over the centuries many times more even as God continued to send prophets to call them back. In so many ways, the story of the woman and the man and the serpent on that fateful day in the Garden of Eden is simply the story of Israel's—and truly, humanity's—history.

A myth, as is oft noted, is not something that never happened but rather something that happens over and over again. Indeed, in each of our lives there is a moment in which we first fail to remain firm in the face of temptation, and in each of our lives, it is a moment that is then repeated many times more.

The Genesis account of the first woman's and man's response to temptation is remarkably perceptive about human nature. The woman (who technically still does not have a name) is approached by a snake. Snakes were common characters in ancient Mesopotamian lore, often playing a similar role to that of Br'er Fox in folklore of the American South—a trickster who enjoys a bit of chaos. In this case, the snake asks a question. It is the first question found in the whole of the Bible: "Did God really say, 'You shall not eat from any of the trees in the garden'?"

The snake's question suggests that God is far more restrictive than is actually the case. God has banned the humans from eating of only the Tree of Knowledge of Good and Evil, not all of the trees. The woman's response suggests that, even before the snake has arrived on the scene, her gaze is already set on this one forbidden tree. She clarifies for the snake that "it is only about the fruit of the tree in the middle of the garden that God said, 'You shall not eat it or even touch it, or else you will die.' But God had never forbidden *touching* the tree, and in Genesis 2, it is only the Tree of Life that is explicitly noted as being in the middle of the garden. One suspects that whether the Tree of Knowledge of Good and Evil *is* in the middle of the garden or not, it has become the center of *her* garden—the tree that has captured her attention.

While never telling the woman what to do, the snake continues to sow doubt in God's word and God's intention, suggesting that eating from this tree won't result in death and God doesn't want her and the man to have knowledge that would make them equal to God. In essence, God doesn't want to share power. Little does she know that there is a form of divine power that is already hers: the capacity to resist the influence of the snake and remain unmoved. Instead, the woman eats of the fruit of the tree and shares the fruit with the man who readily partakes.

Contrast this tale with the gospel accounts of Jesus who at the start of his ministry also finds himself in a space of temptation. Mirroring the story of the Israelites who are wooed through the waters of the Red Sea out into the desert for forty years, Jesus is wooed from the waters of the Jordan River out into the desert for forty days. He has just seen the heavens open and heard a voice announce that he is God's beloved Son, but now Jesus encounters Satan, another clever figure who occasionally appears in the stories of Israel as one who tests the fidelity of God's favored ones under duress.

Satan tempts Jesus three times to see how he will use the power God has shared with him as Son: In his hunger, will he make bread for himself out of stones? Will he test God to catch him as he flings himself from the top of the Temple? Will he enjoy the glory and riches of earthly kings? In each of these temptations, Satan suggests Jesus use the power of his unique role to benefit himself—to assuage his own hunger, to affirm his own belovedness, and to bolster his own status—rather than the cause of the reign of God. We could think of these three temptations as temptations all persons with power will face in a particular way.

Sometimes we treat Jesus's temptations as if they must not have been very serious. After all, it's Jesus we are talking about here, the one born without sin. Surely his attention couldn't be captivated by the dangling fruit of wealth and status. Surely he had a rock-solid sense of his own belovedness and didn't feel the need to bend the laws of nature just because he could. It must have been easy for him to remain firm because he was *just so good*. But as the early twentieth-century British apologist C. S. Lewis notes,

> Only those who try to resist temptation know how strong it is. After all, you find out the strength of [an] army by fighting against it, not by giving in.

> You find out the strength of a wind by trying to walk against it, not by lying down. A man who gives in to temptation after five minutes simply does not know what it would have been like an hour later. . . . We never find out the strength of the evil impulse inside us until we try to fight it; and Christ, because he was the only man who never yielded to temptation, is also the only man who knows to the *full* what temptation means.[1]

Indeed, in the Gospel of Luke, the story of Jesus's temptations in the desert ends with the mysterious line "When the devil had finished every temptation, he departed from him for a time" (Lk 4:13). Luke implies Jesus will continue to face temptation, most especially as he approaches his death. But as one of the earliest Christian hymns proclaims, Jesus "though he was in the form of God, did not regard equality with God something to be grasped" (Phil 2:6). In direct contrast to Eve grasping at divinity in the garden, Jesus fully embraces and accepts his humanity, including the very human experiences of unrealized longing and limitation.

How was it that Jesus managed to remain firm—unchanged and unmoved—under so much pressure? The gospels, especially the Gospel of Luke, paint a picture of Jesus as someone who cultivated a private, interior life that supported his public life. He repeatedly withdraws from the crowd to be with just a few close friends, and then sometimes he withdraws even from his closest friends to spend time alone in prayer. A piece of me is always curious: What were these conversations between Jesus and his Father like? How did they help Jesus remain grounded when surrounded by so many different voices all trying to influence him in so many different ways? The irony is that we likely *do* have a good idea of what these conversations looked like from the prayer that Jesus taught us. We can surmise that the Lord's Prayer was not just something Jesus gave us to memorize but a snapshot of how Jesus himself prayed.

In his prayer, Jesus puts God's will—the coming reign of God—at the very center of his garden. He wants his eyes focused there and nowhere else. He asks for what he needs to keep the reign of God at the heart of everything he does: asking for daily bread, for a spirit of forgiveness, that he not be tested more than what he can handle, and for deliverance from evil. On the night before he dies, we are given an intimate glimpse into Jesus praying this way when twice he says, "Not my will but yours be done"(Lk 22:42) and then wakes his disciples with the admonition, "Pray that you may not undergo the test"(Lk 22:46). Is the fact that this scene takes place in a garden incidental? Unlikely. Jesus is faithful in the same space where the first woman and man were not.

All of us are, of course, called to remain firm like Jesus in the face of temptation. The right use of power in every human's vocation includes both the capacity to change and the capacity to remain unchanged. As a means of cultivating a resistance to temptation, all of us are called to follow Jesus's lead in developing a prayer life and close, trusted relationships with a few people who will tell us the truth when we are headed in the wrong direction. In leadership, though, because the temptations will be so strong and our failing to resist temptations affects so many more people than ourselves, the commitment to prayer and truth-telling in relationships needs to be correspondingly heightened. The more people our lives impact, the greater the responsibility to ground ourselves.

Unfortunately, just as we face some particular temptations as leaders, we also face some particular challenges in remaining grounded. Research shows that people in roles of power have less access to challenging feedback since the feedback they receive often passes through several filters before reaching them and the persons around them are naturally more hesitant to share it.[2] The greater rank one has within an organization, the harder it is to find truth tellers who will give negative or uncomfortable information that could nevertheless be important to have.

Furthermore, research shows that persons who experience power tend to trust their own judgment more highly than persons who experience less power, and they tend to be more optimistic about outcomes.[3] This propensity is not necessarily bad. Leaders need to be able to think outside the box and have the courage to take risks to move their communities in new directions.

If we continually doubt our own judgment, it will be hard for us to play the vital role our communities need us to play. But this same self-confidence also makes it easier for leaders to fall prey to the most insidious temptations those with power face[4]—the irrational belief that this time stones will turn into bread, that because we are so special someone will catch us if we jump, and that it's okay to accommodate the devil just a little bit. Hope is a Christian virtue; unfettered optimism puts one out of contact with reality.

Simply put, the experience of power makes it trickier for us to see what others can see. Unless we are disciplined and intentional in developing a few very honest relationships, we are unlikely to be able to resist the particular temptations we will face as leaders. Spouses and longtime friends can be helpful in this regard, but often we will need to go outside our usual circle of daily relationships to find someone who can be skillfully yet fearlessly frank with us, be that an executive coach, a spiritual director, or a mentor from another institution.

"What I am afraid of with my power is that it will consume me, and my ego and I won't know it," a faith-based diversity, equity, and inclusion consultant relayed to me:

> There is a fine line between being confident and being egotistical. I've watched people who once they get known and get more power, they go off

a cliff. I want the right people around me who
will help me to stay grounded. . . . I have a strong
spiritual director who loves me and sees me and
calls me out. I also have close friends whom I trust
and who are not intimidated by me. Friends who
will not just tell me I am great and beautiful, but
will also tell me when I was "off," unkind.

Yet, as she and others I interviewed noted, the gift of
accountability partners still must be complemented
by time alone in prayer. "In the gospels, you see Jesus
heal someone or feed five thousand, and people would
gather around him and want to make him king," a
bishop commented to me. "Jesus had a way of taking
care of that by disappearing. When he'd done a big
miracle, they'd have to go looking for him because he'd
gone off by himself to pray. I also disappear at times. I,
too, need to slip out the side door sometimes and fight
against the inclination to be noticed." Another bishop
commented, "I try to think 'relationship-identity-
mission' in that order. If I maintain my relationship
with God in prayer, then I realize that I am first a sheep
of the Good Shepherd. My mission as shepherd in the
diocese has to flow out of that identity. I think we most
get ourselves in trouble when mission comes first and
then our identity is formed by what we *do* and what
people say. That's when problems emerge."

Business leadership consultant Julie Diamond
notes something similar when she acknowledges

the most common ethical failing among leaders is using the power that comes from their position in the community to meet their own internal needs and desires—for love, meaning, sex, wealth, adulation, and control.[5] Ultimately, it is only God who can meet our deepest needs. Taking a couple of minutes each day for centering prayer[6] or "Espacio" (as we will hear about below) can help make us more aware of what our internal needs and desires are, and give us a way to entrust them to God's care. A popular preacher I interviewed observed, "I have to do a lot of work with my inner self. Here I am trying to convince others they are loved by God, yet there are parts of me that don't feel loved. If I don't spend time grounding myself in my identity as God's beloved . . . well, I don't like thinking what could happen."

In the end, what keeps us unmoved in times of temptation is a deep-rootedness in knowledge, not knowledge of "good and evil," but of ourselves as fully human and forever loved. Much of the power we enjoy in life will be specific to a particular context: In comparison to this group of people, I am wealthy. In comparison to this society's standards, I am beautiful. On this social media platform, I have lots of followers. But when power comes to us from a context—in essence, outside of us—it will always leave us feeling vulnerable because a change in employment or health or popularity could take our sense of power away in an instant. And when we are vulnerable, we are much more susceptible to influence.

But when our power is grounded in a private, interior life—a life that cultivates integrity and authenticity—we find ourselves tapping into a source of power that change of circumstance can never take away. "I have a favorite verse from the Jerusalem Bible," a provincial team leader of a women's religious community told me. "It says, 'May you be given power through the Spirit that your hidden self may grow strong' (Eph 3:16). That hidden self is the essence of who I most truly am. That's the power I want to rely on." It's the power we should all want to rely on. It's the most stable, enduring power that there is.

Companion for the Journey:
Madeleine Sophie Barat

Madeleine Sophie Barat—known as Sophie—was born in the midst of a firestorm. Quite literally, she came into the world two months premature after her mother went into early labor during a fire that devastated her hometown of Joigny, France. Fearful for her tiny life, her brother Louis—then only eleven years old—rushed her before sunrise to the local parish to be baptized. Barat remained frail throughout her life, prone to frequent illness. She never grew above four foot ten.

But Barat was also born *into* the midst of a firestorm. Her childhood witnessed the economic collapse that led to the outbreak of the French Revolution when she was ten years old. Her later teen years were spent in hiding in Paris with Louis, now a young priest, who had only narrowly escaped the guillotine during Robespierre's Reign of Terror. Events that feature prominently in history books—the conquests of Napoleon, the restoration of the Bourbons, and the July Monarchy—are all events that Barat personally lived through.

It is no wonder one of Barat's early hopes was to become a Carmelite nun, withdrawn from the chaos and violence of the world. But at the urging of Louis and his friend Joseph Varin, Barat instead joined a tiny emerging community of women devoted to the Sacred Heart of Jesus with the vision of healing the violence of the time through living lives of love in the ministry of education. After six years with the community as it went through several permutations and names, Barat emerged as the leader of the Society of the Sacred Heart in 1806. She was twenty-seven. It was a role that she would remain steadfast in for almost six decades.

Overseeing a new, rapidly growing community in the aftermath of the French Revolution was not an easy task, as evidenced in the approximately fourteen thousand letters that we have by Barat from her time of leadership. The correspondence offers a window into the innumerable requests Barat received to start

schools and how she was constantly concerned with
the quality of teachers she had to fill these roles. Many
of the women who joined the community were wealthy
and well educated but disinclined to pull in the same
direction. "You are only obedient when you are asleep,"
she wrote to one of her closest collaborators.[7]

There were constant debates about whether to
center the community in France or Rome, whether
to observe the cloister or be out more in the world,
and whether to focus on boarding schools for the
elite or day schools for the poor. It was hard to know
what voices to listen to and which to resist. "What a
life I lead . . . my last days are full of wrangling and
quarrels!" she confided to a sympathetic bishop.[8]

Perhaps the most difficult antagonist Barat
had to face each day, though, was the voice inside
her own head. Barat had been raised in a family
steeped in Jansenism, a spirituality that emphasized
the sinfulness of persons and the judgment of God.
Jansenism encouraged frequent confession, but
infrequent communion, as one was never quite worthy.
In her years spent under Louis's influence, Barat had
become excessively scrupulous and even in her later
years continually doubted her own abilities, powerless
over her own thoughts. "[Her] pains, scruples, and
worries . . . are partly due to her temperament and
partly due to the false guidance she has been following
for a long time," her spiritual director Joseph-Marie
Favre noted of her. "But they are due most of all to the

devil who aims solely to make her waste precious time by useless self-occupation and by making her examine her conscience endlessly, like a squirrel going round in circles."[9]

For years, Favre worked to help Barat see that the image of the Sacred Heart that featured so prominently in the French politics of her century was more than a sign of resistance to the revolution and the chaos it had wrought. It was an invitation to meet a gentle and loving God who readily forgave and wanted to draw near in Eucharist—a God who wanted to ground her and give her peace. Whereas earlier in life Barat saw all the problems of leadership as an obstacle to her prayer, Favre led her on a journey to pause and pray with her problems. She did not need to hide from the world but, as Barat would later write, "unite solitude to the work we do, and counter this whirlwind with a deep cavern where the soul can take refuge. . . . For us this cavern in the rock is the Heart of Jesus!"[10]

With time, Barat learned to become a contemplative in the midst of the firestorm, less reactive and more responsive. As a result, she became gentler with others. "What is done is done. Let us stop worrying about it anymore now!" she writes in 1859. "The past should be left to the compassion of Jesus Christ. Besides, we did not have enough light at the time and so our mistakes are less culpable."[11] She also became gentler with herself. "People are often hard on leaders," she acknowledged toward the end of her life, expecting from them unwavering virtue and an iron constitution, and they are blamed for everything, when, like everyone else, they are frail humans! This attitude was a source of suffering to me for some time until I realized the impossibility of pleasing everyone and of being more than human. This is my secret for peace, and I share it with you.[12]

At the time of Barat's death in May 1865, over 3,300 women belonged to the Society of the Sacred Heart, serving schools in Europe, North Africa, and North and South America. At this point, there are over 150 Sacred Heart schools in forty-one countries around the globe.[13] As a way of honoring Barat's legacy, a common practice across these schools is "Espacio"[14] or making "space" for several minutes of silence in the school day to reground oneself in calm, no matter the pressures and temptations of life.

For Reflection

- This chapter introduces a new definition of power as the ability to resist change rather than make change. How do you see this new definition of power exercised in your leadership?

- Some would argue that the temptations Jesus faced are temptations all leaders face. Some would say that each leader has their own unique temptations they will need to confront. To what extent do you identify with Jesus's temptations? Are there others that you would name as more difficult?

- Describe a time when you've been tempted to use your role as a leader to meet your own interests rather than the mission of the organization/ ministry you lead. What were the outcomes in this situation?

- Which relationships do you most depend on to keep you grounded as a leader? Which spiritual practices?

- What insight do you glean from Madeleine Sophie Barat's story concerning the spirituality of power, especially as it relates to remaining steadfast in mission and firm in the face of temptation?

8. Exercising the Power to Ask Questions

When they heard the sound of the LORD God walking about in the garden at the breezy time of the day, the man and his wife hid themselves from the LORD God among the trees of the garden. The LORD God then called to the man and asked him: Where are you? He answered, "I heard you in the garden; but I was afraid, because I was naked, so I hid." Then God asked: Who told you that you were naked? Have you eaten from the tree of which I had forbidden you to eat? The man replied, "The woman whom you put here with me—she gave me fruit from the tree, so I ate it." The LORD God then asked the woman: What is this you have done?

—Genesis 3:8–13

If the first question in the Bible belongs to the snake, the second question in the Bible belongs to God. The man and woman are not to be found where expected. Having eaten from the Tree of Knowledge of Good and

Evil, they are now aware of their nakedness and hiding from God. God comes looking for them, crying out, "Where are you?"

Twentieth-century Jewish scholar Abraham Joshua Heschel notes that this question from the opening pages of Genesis sets the stage for the whole drama of human history that will unfold in the pages to come. We often go to the Bible with our own questions about God. We read scripture as a way of seeking the divine and find companions in the ancient characters found there. Heschel says that we have the main plot line wrong, however. The Bible is not the story of humanity's search for God so much as the story of God's search for humanity. "This is the mystery paradox of Biblical faith," Heschel states. "God is pursuing man. It is as if God were unwilling to be alone, and He had chosen man to serve Him. . . . All of human history as described in the Bible may be summarized in one phrase: God is in search of man."[1] God seeks what the Bible refers to as a "servant of the Lord." In Heschel's description, this was not a "slave" as in the ancient Mesopotamian sense of one who would meet the gods' whims but rather a human willing to truly be God's image on earth and live the human vocation.

As Adam steps out scantily clad from his hiding spot, he has clearly *not* been living his true human vocation, and God follows with a series of additional questions: "Who told you that you were naked? Did you eat from the tree from which I had forbidden you to eat?" And then to the woman, "What is this you have done?" Over the centuries, the rabbis have had a field day with this scene and what God's act of continued questioning reveals to us about God.

The medieval French Talmudist Ralbag notes that God's questioning of the woman and man reminds us that before we condemn anyone, we should first confront them in person to see if there is an explanation. "For though God was fully familiar with all the facts, He did not punish them until He conversed with them and afforded them the opportunity to reveal any excuse they might have had."[2] The Midrash Aggadah also emphasizes that God (being God) would have already known what had happened but wanted to give the woman and man a chance to take ownership for their actions and repent:

> God opened the dialogue to give Adam the opportunity to acknowledge his sin and be pardoned. But Adam did not confess. Instead, . . . he hurled against God the very kindness which God had shown him, the gift of Eve, by implying that God had caused him to sin by giving him that woman. . . . Seeing that Adam had not expressed regret, God turned to Eve saying "*what is this that you have done?*" in the hope that she would confess so He could forgive them both. But she did not do this.[3]

The rabbis seem to be lifting up two important aspects of God's questioning. First, even God pauses to seek additional information (or at least perspective) before arriving at a conclusion. Second, sometimes questions might also serve the ones being queried, giving *them* a chance to pause and reflect in the hope that it might lead to insight—and ultimately change—on their part.

While not often considered, asking questions is one of the ways God exercises power, not only in Genesis but also throughout scripture. Consider God's conversations with Abraham, Moses, Job, and Jeremiah. In every generation, God seeks out and forms "servants of the Lord" largely by posing questions to them. The whole rabbinic method of reading and studying scripture mirrors God's practice, taking every word of the scriptural text as inexhaustibly revelatory if asked questions from multiple different angles. In Judaism, a good question is valued even more highly than a good answer. Questions are considered the best tool for learning.

It's no surprise then that the first words ever attributed to Jesus in his youth are questions. When he is found in the Temple after a tense three-day search, Mary and Joseph discover him "sitting in the midst of the teachers, listening to them and asking them questions" (Lk 2:46). It sounds as if Jesus is learning from the rabbis, which is likely, but given that asking questions *is* the rabbinical mode of teaching, it indicates that they were also learning from him—that at the age of twelve, he was already a rabbi himself.

Throughout his ministry, Jesus engaged others by way of questions. In the four gospels, Jesus is recorded asking 308 questions. By way of contrast, he is asked 183 questions, and of that 183, he directly answers only a handful. (Depending on what you consider to be "direct," the number is between three and eight.[4]) This means Jesus is at least forty times more likely to ask a question than he is to give a clear answer to one, prompting one professor to quip to his class of budding theologians, "Just remember: Jesus is the question to all of your answers."[5]

Like God in the Garden of Eden, Jesus uses questions to serve multiple potential purposes. Sometimes he does seem to genuinely want to understand a situation better and get important information: "What are you looking for?" (Jn 1:38). "What do you want me to do for you?" (Mt 20:32). But many of his questions are more rhetorical in nature. He uses them to steer a lesson in a particular direction while keeping hearers engaged. "Can the wedding guests mourn as long as the bridegroom is with them?" (Mt 9:15). "Which one of you would hand his son a stone when he asks for a loaf of bread?" (Mt 7:9). He could have taught in lecture format and perhaps made his point even more quickly by stating, "Worry is useless." Instead he asks, "Can any of you by worrying add a single moment to your life-span?" (Mt 6:27). A question requires a response on the part of the hearers, if not aloud, then at least in their minds.

Often Jesus's questions were open-ended and may not have evoked an immediate answer but would have continued to echo in hearers' minds long after he had moved on to the next town: "What could one give in exchange for his life?" (Mk 8:37). "What is the kingdom of God like?" (Lk 13:18). Yet sometimes, as in the Garden of Eden, his questions put people on the spot. These questions could be awkward and might have identified dynamics many would be too polite to raise: "Do you see this woman?" (Lk 7:44). "Where is your faith?" (Lk 8:25). "Why do you not understand what I am saying?" (Jn 8:43). In the gospels of Matthew and Mark, even Jesus's last words take the form of a question, perhaps the most difficult question of all: "My God, my God, why have you forsaken me?" (Mk 15:34; Mt 27:46).

Asking questions is part of being human, starting at around two and a half to three years of age. If we first start to communicate by way of gesture and then by mastering the names of things, shortly after we begin to put words together, we begin to ask questions: Why is the bird lying on the sidewalk? Why do I have to take a nap? (While I was writing this very paragraph sitting on a park bench, a preschooler walked up to me and queried, "What are you doing?") Questioning is the way we learn and grow in the world, the way we initiate conversation and connect to others. It is hard to imagine any conversation of interest going on for very long without the asking of questions.

The freedom to ask questions, however, is relative to one's power. Those who experience more power in a relationship will feel freer to ask for more information. They will feel freer to raise hard or awkward questions. And they will feel freer to ask rhetorical questions. "Could you justify these expenses for me?" is a totally acceptable question for the manager to ask of the supervisee, but the supervisee would hesitate to ask that same question of the manager. Many a parent has uttered with exasperation, "Do you think money grows on trees?" but if children asked that in return, they may well end up in their room till dinner. This power dynamic that is present in querying presents a debacle for leaders. On the one hand, asking questions is critical to the exercise of holy and healthy leadership. On the other hand, leaders' questions can easily affect others in ways not necessarily intended.

Almost every book on leadership encourages leaders to ask lots of questions. As noted in the last chapter, persons in positions of power often assume that they know and understand more than they do. The information that comes to them has often been filtered by others before it arrives to their attention, and they are more likely to trust their own perception than persons with less power.[6] While asking questions to glean information is important for anyone who wants to learn, leaders will need to be especially attentive to asking for information that might not naturally come their way or that they might overlook the importance of. "I know I need to get better at asking better questions," a bishop reported to me. "I need to learn how to frame questions so that they open the door to more conversation rather than shut it."

A helpful practice among leaders is the "one thing question."[7] Rather than saying, "I have an open door policy. Feel free to tell me anything you think I need to hear," leaders need to ask for information people may not feel inclined to give those in power. But they need to ask for it in small, manageable bites: What's one thing you see me doing (or not doing) that is getting in my way? What's one thing that I could change that you think would make a difference for the staff? What's one idea you have to make this project even better? What's one thing you think might get in the way of this event being a success? What's one thing you think I should be paying attention to that I might be missing? Asking for only one thing versus everything allows the other to focus on what is most important from their perspective and not be overwhelmed by trying to give a comprehensive assessment.

Because those with power have more leeway to ask questions, it will often fall to leaders to ask the more awkward or difficult ones lest they never be asked. Just as Jesus raised to the surface underlying dynamics, leaders need to find the courage to ask what others are likely wondering but are nervous to talk about: Should we name closing the school as an option? How is racism alive in our organization? Is clericalism playing a role in how we are functioning as a council? Is there an elephant in the room we are avoiding?

It is not that as leaders we will necessarily feel comfortable raising hard questions, but we are likely to feel more comfortable than anyone else in the room will. When interviewed, a religious convert who has now become a social media influencer said to me, "I think the first book everyone should be introduced to when they join the church is the book of Job." Her newfound faith compels her to raise tough social and doctrinal issues online, but her choice to do so has come with a great deal of tension. "I would love to hone the skill of asking hard questions in a daring yet compassionate way."

From an ethics lens, the concern about asking lots of questions (including hard ones) isn't that it opens the leader to a world of discomfort (though it will) but what it asks of the other. Even well-intentioned questions can backfire. Curiosity can be experienced by the other as invasive. A request for suggestions about how to improve can be perceived as a request for uncompensated labor, giving away one's ideas for free. A conversation meant to understand better what happened can feel like an accusation.

A leader who works diligently on reconciling relationships with First Nations people relayed, "I've learned that for me as a white person trying to be friendly and interested by asking a lot of questions about another's heritage can feel like I'm asking for information that I've not earned and should only be shared after years of being in relationship. Better just to sit silent until they ask me a question." In tender situations, many leaders are now learning to step back and first check: "Is it okay if I ask you about . . . ?" "Is it important to this conversation that I understand . . . ?" Linked to this more hesitant stance is the realization that those who enjoy more power are also freer *not* to answer a question, whereas those who experience less power will have a harder time responding "no comment." The teacher who doesn't want to answer a question moves the class on to another topic. The student who doesn't want to answer a question fails the test.

A separate yet related concern has to do with the righteous use of rhetorical questions. Unlike questions meant to learn more information, open up conversation, and foster a sense of connection, rhetorical questions are meant to guide the other toward a particular conclusion. When the printing press first came into being, printers used a reverse question mark symbol at the end of rhetorical questions to indicate that such questions were a different category of speech.[8] Now readers have no such clue.

To say something is a rhetorical question doesn't mean it is a bad question. As noted earlier, rhetorical questions are an age-old teaching tool, and Jesus was fond of them. But rhetorical questions raise interesting ethical concerns when there is an intellectual or linguistic power differential. Persons who are not as academically learned or don't "have a way with words" can end up feeling tongue-tied or unable to get a word in edgewise. The wisdom of age and life can sometimes have a hard time getting into the conversation.

Moreover, if the one asking rhetorical questions doesn't have a strong commitment to seeking truth, the attractiveness of the argument alone can lead hearers in a dangerous direction, as populist political movements throughout history have proven. Leaders whose "power over" comes from their mastery of language are highly susceptible to sophistry, the sin of loving the argument more than the truth. "I know I can fill a room and use words well," a popular speaker admitted to me. "I can engage people's emotions and can elicit a response from them. It is what makes a good preacher, but it is also what makes a good snake oil salesman." Her response reminded me that the first question each of us wakes up to in the morning when we open our newsfeed is still often that of the serpent.

In this realm as in all the others, the exercise of holy and healthy power is a balancing act. We engage questions seeking more truth, with the hope of being able to offer more truth. We do so not always knowing if we've got the right question to ask—the one that will do more good than harm. We do so not always knowing if this is the right moment to ask it or whether we are the right person to be doing so. Yet we try to exercise this power of questioning in simultaneously bold and careful ways. To paraphrase the famous quote from the poet Rainer Maria Rilke, we live the questions we have about questions now with the hope that someday in the future, we will gradually, without even knowing it, live our way into the answer.[9]

Companion for the Journey: **Thea Bowman**

Thea Bowman was all about asking hard questions. "Where are you right now?" she would ask her grade school students.[10] "Where do you find that in the text? How does that prove your idea?" her college literature students remember her asking.[11] "Why do you do that?" she challenged participants who self-segregated during social time at a conference on intercultural sensitivity.[12] "Now why can't we use some of that kind of acumen that could get people into space . . . to figure out a welfare system that is real and that works?"[13] she prodded a journalist. And then perhaps her most famous questions of all, asked of the bishops of the United States Catholic Conference: "What does it mean to be Black and Catholic? It means I come to my church fully functioning. That doesn't frighten you, does it?"[14] The Church continues to wrestle with these questions to this day.

Thea Bowman was born Bertha Bowman in Yazoo City, Mississippi, in 1937. Her father, a doctor in Canton, insisted that her mother stay with relatives there because Yazoo City had a hospital that would admit Black patients whereas Canton, thirty miles away, did not. The beloved only child of older parents, Bowman reveled in religion—particularly "old-time religion"—from her earliest years. She attended a variety of local churches before asking to be baptized a Catholic at the age of nine. She enrolled in the first Catholic school in the area, Holy Child Jesus School, the year that it opened and immediately fell in love with the Franciscan Sisters of Perpetual Adoration who taught there. At the age of fifteen, she begged her parents to allow her to join the predominantly German-Irish congregation based nine hundred miles away in La Crosse, Wisconsin. She was the community's first Black member and, for the whole of her life, remained its only Black member.

Bowman, who took the religious name Thea upon becoming a novice in 1956, enjoyed life in her new community but also struggled. Her style of worship and expression, even the food of her childhood, were foreign to the convent. She felt she had to deny who she was as a Black woman to fit into the mostly white congregation. Her experience was not unusual among Black women joining religious life—a fact she realized only later when pursuing advanced studies in English literature at the Catholic University of America in

Washington, DC. Here she had the chance to meet other Black women religious and become one of the first members of the National Black Sisters Conference in 1968. She began to ask new questions about how to best lift up the beauty of her heritage.

Upon finishing her doctorate, Bowman returned to La Crosse to teach at Viterbo University, a college sponsored by her congregation. She integrated Black literature and music into the curriculum. She launched a Hallelujah choir that sang Black spirituals. She became chair of the English department. Yet despite her popularity and success as an academic, she felt a tug to return home to care for her aging parents.

In 1978, she moved back to Canton where she was immediately tapped by Bishop Joseph Brunini to become the diocese's first consultant for intercultural awareness. She sought to open people's eyes to the diverse gifts different cultures bring to the Church, beginning with her own. When leading gatherings, she would offer a sense of that richness through singing, dancing, storytelling, and preaching. Her most frequent questions in front of a crowd were, "Are you with me, Church?"[15] and "Can I get you to say 'Amen'?"[16] Others beyond Mississippi began to take notice of her captivating presentations and presence. Soon she was crisscrossing the country as a coveted speaker at conferences, graduations, and concerts. She became a summer faculty member at the Institute for Black Catholic Studies in New Orleans.

The year 1984 was particularly difficult for Bowman as she lost both parents and was diagnosed with breast cancer within a couple of months. Yet it also crystallized her focus: "I've always asked God for the grace to live until I die."[17] And live she did. Over the next six years, she came more deeply in contact with her African roots through visits to Kenya and Tanzania. She worked on *Lead Me; Guide Me*—a hymnal for Black Catholics. She prepared a resource for ministers called *Families: Black and Catholic, Catholic and Black*. She was interviewed by Mike Wallace on *60 Minutes* and recorded two musical albums.

She seemed to be everywhere all at once with her consistent message: "Black is beautiful! White is beautiful! Brown is beautiful! . . . All the colors and hues in between that God made us are beautiful. Straight hair is beautiful! Kinky hair is beautiful!" After being treated with chemotherapy, she would sometimes remove her headwrap to add, "Bald is beautiful!"[18]

Bowman is perhaps most remembered as the woman who brought the US Catholic bishops to their feet to sing together "We Shall Overcome." Her speech at their June 1989 gathering challenged *them* with the same question she asked her grade school students, an echo of God's question in Eden: Where are you? What are you doing to invite Black Catholics into greater participation in the Church? How are you recognizing the gifts of Black culture? Why does so much beauty continue to remain hidden? Bowman's talk synthesized all that she had come to celebrate about her people's history and urged the overcoming of racism not "someday" but "today."[19]

Bowman died nine months later, early in the morning of March 30, 1990. Having asked so many powerful questions interrogating the Church's inclusion of Black Americans, her last question was "Let me go, okay?"[20] In fall 2018, the US Conference of Catholic Bishops voted to support the cause for Bowman's canonization. It was one more step toward embracing the beauty of being both Black and Catholic.

For Reflection

- The first question God asks in the Bible is also one that Thea Bowman regularly asked her students: "Where are you?" How would you answer that question right now in terms of living your own call in life?

- Which of Jesus's questions from the gospels has most captured your attention and stuck with you over time? What observations do you have about Jesus's way of using questions?

- What best practices have you developed for yourself to ensure you take time to listen and get more information before arriving at a judgment?

- Do you find yourself using questions, including rhetorical questions, as a way of leading (in the classroom, from the pulpit, in a staff meeting, online, etc.)? What are the advantages and disadvantages of this teaching methodology from your experience?

- What insight do you glean from Thea Bowman's story concerning the spirituality of power, especially as it relates to asking good questions?

9. Exercising the Power to Judge

To the woman he said: I will intensify your toil in childbearing; in pain you shall bring forth children. Yet your urge shall be for your husband, and he shall rule over you. To the man he said: Because you listened to your wife and ate from the tree about which I commanded you, You shall not eat from it, Cursed is the ground because of you! In toil you shall eat its yield all the days of your life. . . . By the sweat of your brow you shall eat bread, Until you return to the ground, from which you were taken; For you are dust, and to dust you shall return.

—Genesis 3:16–17, 19

Then the LORD God said: See! The man has become like one of us, knowing good and evil! Now, what if he also reaches out his hand to take fruit from the tree of life, and eats of it and lives forever? The LORD God therefore banished him from the garden of

Eden, to till the ground from which he had been taken. He expelled the man, stationing the cherubim and the fiery revolving sword east of the garden of Eden, to guard the way to the tree of life.

—Genesis 3:22–24

One of the hardest passages to read in all of scripture is the passage where God describes the world that the man and woman will know now that "their eyes are open." In some ways, these are the realities that all humans awaken to as they move into adulthood: the world is a place of strife and pain. It is not the Eden we might have known as a child. Animals bite. Relationships are not all friendly, transparent, and simple. There is not only "power to" but now also "power over" and the experience of powerlessness. Death becomes a reality; and immortality, no longer a possibility. As a result, we now know fear and hence are subject to coercion. Once "knowledge" is gained, there is no way to go back to the world where we were before, nor to the relationship with God that we had before.

For our ancestors in faith, it was probably that last part—changed relationship with God—that was the most painful realization of all. The scene of the expulsion from the garden echoed their own experience of the destruction of the Temple in Jerusalem and exile to Babylon. The Temple—also entered from the east—had been guarded by images of cherubim at the approach to the inner sanctuary. These human-headed winged lions were the traditional protectors of sacred places throughout the ancient Near East. The Tree of Life would have been one way to refer to the seven-branched candelabra known as a menorah, central to Temple life. For those who first wrote down the Genesis story, the Temple had been like an Eden, a place where they had walked with God, dwelt with God, and all was in right relationship. Losing the Temple and being driven out of Jerusalem had been like a death. In this new world, they could not know God as they had earlier.[1]

The whole conclusion of Genesis 3 feels so unfair. Why couldn't God simply chalk up the eating of the forbidden fruit as a beginner's mistake and show mercy? Why did the Temple need to have been destroyed and a precious way of life lost? Couldn't we go back to a more innocent age? Where is the God of second chances?

We are not the first to ask these questions. Jewish midrash has considered them as well. Midrash suggests that before our own world was created, God created others. One was based purely on justice, and anyone who did wrong was punished with no chance for redemption. It was a harsh and joyless world and did not please God. So God then fashioned a world based solely on forgiveness and compassion. People

saw their neighbors getting away with every sort of
wicked behavior and began to imitate their ways. God
was not pleased with this world either. And so, finally,
God created our own world grounded on the principles
of both justice and mercy.[2]

The world of justice and mercy described in
scripture is not unlike one that psychologists lift up
when describing a healthy home. The most secure, well-
adjusted children are those whose parents or caregivers
create a loving, stable environment where there are
clear and consistent expectations appropriate to the
child's age. It is important that the child knows that the
boundaries of this environment will not disintegrate
simply because they are tested. If the adult gives in
or becomes upset when the child throws a temper
tantrum, the child will end up feeling less secure and
loved, not more, and the child will keep testing to
figure out where the boundaries really are.

"One succinct definition of love is 'always seeking
the highest good for another,'" states Christian
psychologist Eileen Schmitz. "Theologically, this has
been God's focus for humanity from creation onward.
At times, God's search for the highest good for God's
people required the application of justice—at other
times, the application of mercy. But with God, there
is no mercy without justice and no justice without
mercy."[3]

Judgment is a term with lots of negative conno-
tations. At a most basic level, it simply describes the

capacity to put together the facts of a situation to arrive at a conclusion about the worthiness of a statement, behavior, idea, project, and so forth. Judgments are what we use to determine our actions. Everyone makes them all the time; indeed everyone has to make them in the course of daily living. But power magnifies the potential impact of one's judgments on others. With power, the decisions one makes come into being, whether the other party agrees with the judgment or not. Hence the language of judgment when linked with power carries a certain weight or heaviness. Even though one could very well be "judged worthy," when we talk about feeling "judged," we rarely describe it as a positive experience. Rather, we associate it with being misunderstood, critiqued, punished, or held accountable to a standard that we do not share. On the receiving end, judgment rarely *feels* just and almost never feels merciful.

This is likely why the power to judge is the power Christian leaders feel least comfortable talking about. The popular perception of Christian leaders in media is that judging is a task that we relish, that preachers love to proclaim hell, fire, and damnation; that schoolteachers enjoy carrying around a ruler; and that online apologists thrive on holding heretics accountable. There are some Christian leaders who do match this description, and that is certainly problematic. But there are many more who hesitate to exercise judgment at all, or when they do, exercise it only with great personal angst and a lot of second guessing. The absence of a willingness to exercise judgment as a leader comes with its own challenges. It is one of the reasons so many forms of bad, even abusive, behavior are allowed to fester in Christian communities. Where one falls on this spectrum of comfort with the power of judging is surely affected by one's personal disposition, but also by how one thinks about Jesus.

The picture of Jesus and judgment is a complicated one. Many still tend to think about the "God of the Old Testament" as being a harsh judge bent on justice and the "God of the New Testament" as being all about love and mercy, with Jesus representing the latter. It almost sounds as if there are two different gods. A more nuanced and complete picture of the Bible acknowledges that there is one God who is love from beginning to end.

As described by Schmitz, this one God's love has been exercised in history both as justice and mercy, based on what is most needed by the beloved at that moment. Jesus's life and ministry reflect both faces of this divine love. At his birth, Jesus is hailed by the angels as one who will bring peace, and yet later he says, "Do you think that I have come to establish peace on the earth? No" (Lk 12:51). He preached about the prodigal son whose past was forgiven by his father. He also preached about the foolish bridesmaids being locked out of the wedding feast. In Jesus's teaching, the tax collector goes home justified, and yet the glutton who dines with Lazarus outside his door can't be redeemed. He restores the widow of Nain's son to his mother's arms, and he also says he has come to divide "a mother against her daughter and a daughter against her mother" (Lk 12:53). It is all true. All of the same man.

One of the most difficult lines from the gospels for leaders to reconcile is Matthew 7:1: "Stop judging, that you may not be judged" For some, this passage is easily balanced out with other injunctions to speak the truth. They are compelled to let people know what is right and wrong regardless of whether they want to hear it. For others, however, Matthew 7:1 is nearly paralyzing. "Judging is God's task, not mine," they will say, "Who am I to judge?" Most of us are probably somewhere in the middle, realizing that sometimes we do need to take strong stands on issues. Sometimes we do need to enforce boundaries and issue consequences. Sometimes we need to let someone go from their position for cause. And then sometimes we need to withhold judgment and wait for more information. Sometimes we do need to let things go. Sometimes we need to forgive and give another chance. Stuck in this in-between space, most of us aren't sure that we are ever getting it quite right. Said one pastor I interviewed:

> Any number of nights when I'm doing my examen, I realized I've erred on the side of mercy

and compassion. . . . I sometimes wonder if I've
been a little bit too kind. I work really hard at
building people up so that they feel empowered
to make good decisions. Yet there have been nights
where I'm lying in bed and thought, Ach, it would
have been better if I'd said something was out of
line. I should have called the person to conversion.
And I have to ask God to be merciful to me and
be very, very kind to them because they are only
doing what I said to do. It's funny when you are
willing to take it on the chin with the Divine for
someone else, but I don't know how else to go
about doing ministry, right?

And yet a former dean in higher education admitted:

I think, looking back, I was probably too harsh.
I am remembering when I let a faculty member
go for a single offense. It involved an act of
very poor judgment on his part. From an HR
perspective, I had to do it. But he lost his whole
career in academia. Sometimes I wonder, could
we have figured out another way to work out a
reconciliation?

Given the ambiguity many of us feel related to the
power of judgment, how does one practice judgment
in a holy and healthy way as a leader?

First, we need to recognize that whatever Jesus
meant by "Do not judge," he could not have meant
"Anything goes." It feels important to read this line

in the context of those that immediately follow about the "measure with which you measure" being the "measure" that will be used to measure you and the command to remove "the beam in your own eye" before trying to remove "the splinter in your brother's eye" (Mt 7:2–3). Jesus seems to be clarifying his initial statement by acknowledging that concerning judgment, we should judge by the same standards as we ourselves would wish to be judged, and that if we are in a position of judgment over others, we have a special responsibility to be aware of our own issues.

But judgment itself is necessary for human life, and the capacity to make good judgments for the sake of a community's life is constitutive of good leadership. Like parents on the home front, our task as leaders is about establishing a loving, stable environment for people, which includes having boundaries that don't disintegrate when tested. Jesus himself made plenty of judgments.

Furthermore, Jesus entrusted his disciples with the "power of the keys"—generally understood as the power to make judgments about what behaviors will be tolerated within the life of the community and what behaviors will not (Mt 16:19; Mt 18:18; Jn 20:23). It is hard to imagine he would have so explicitly given this power if he didn't expect it to be used. Powers, like lamps, are not meant to be hidden under bushel baskets. While only a few of us reading this book technically hold the "power of the keys" in a formal ecclesial sense, many of us do participate in this power within the institutions we serve as managers and policy-makers. We can imagine Jesus expects us, like the first disciples, to use the power of judgment to protect not the institution itself (that could be dangerous and lead to the cover-up of abuse) but the mission for which the institution was founded. He expects us to make judgments that best serve the people the institution was founded to serve.

In order to exercise this "power of the keys" well, we will need to acknowledge that a door that is always open isn't really a door but a passageway, and a door that is always shut isn't really a door but a wall. If we are skilled at only the application of justice *or* the application of mercy, we will not be able to lead well in *this* world that God created, versus the two imaginary worlds found in the Midrash. We need to know how to apply both justice and mercy and how to discern when to swing in which direction. "Prayer helps. Age helps. Years of experience help. You get a better gut sense over time," the former dean told me.

Having discernment partners also helps. The novice director of a women's religious community relayed:

> Sometimes my codirector and I were not always on the same page when we had to send someone home. She was always more optimistic about people's capacity to change. I remember her once

saying, "I think we've turned a corner," and me replying, "I don't think there are any more corners to turn." But I very much appreciated having someone to make the decision with so that it wasn't me alone, not knowing if it was just my issues at play.

For better or worse, the constraints of the circumstances also often have a role to play. "I think lots of times, people assume we are trying to make the best discernment from among multiple good options," a college administrator told me. "Most days, I'm just trying to make the least bad decision from among multiple awful options." None of us live in Eden.

And perhaps that is the most important fact to keep in mind when engaging the power of judgment as a leader. Eating from the Tree of the Knowledge of Good and Evil once upon a time did not really give us as much knowledge about good and evil as we might hope. Or perhaps we can tell what is good from what is bad, but we still might not always know what to do about it in the exercise of our office. The only thing we can do is humbly accept that the world isn't Eden and that we must adapt our leadership to meet the needs of the world in which we live—one that needs both justice and mercy, as we ourselves do.

Companion for the Journey:
Antonio de Montesinos

"This may be news to you, you may never have heard
my voice before, the most severe, the most demanding,
the most terrible for you to listen to, [but] I have to tell
you that you are all in a state of mortal sin. You now
live in it, and you will die in it."[4] It was not your typical
Advent preaching with cozy images of a mother with
child or a light shining in the darkness, but it certainly
remains one of the most memorable.

The year was 1511, just a few weeks before
Christmas. The setting was the island of Hispaniola
in the Caribbean—now Haiti and the Dominican
Republic. The crowd was large as all the landowners
and government officials were personally invited.
Even the governor, Christopher Columbus's son, was
present. And the preacher was Antonio de Montesinos,
one of the first four Dominican friars to arrive on the
island a year earlier. He and his Dominican brothers
had come from Spain to evangelize the local Taino
population but instead found themselves horrified
by the way that fellow Spaniards were treating the
Taino—forcing them into mining, separating families,
and treating them as slaves. The friars decided that
a stern word of judgment needed to be spoken and
chose Montesinos to speak on their behalf, as he was
considered their most powerful preacher.

When Montesinos stepped into the pulpit, like John the Baptist, he minced no words: "I am the voice of one crying in the wilderness," he proclaimed.

> Tell me, what gives you the right to subject these Indians to such an atrocious and horrible slavery? What authority have you for waging war on these people who used to live peacefully and without aggression on their own lands? . . . They once flourished in large communities, but a great many are now dead and forgotten as a result of your actions.[5]

Those present were shocked. A listener later recorded that Montesinos left his congregation "aghast": "Some of them were almost fainting, others petrified, a few repentant, but not one of them fully convinced."[6] A number of the government leaders assembled that afternoon outside the Dominicans' residence demanding that Montesinos be sent out to them. The prior, twenty-nine-year-old Pedro de Cordoba, came out to meet them, noting that the preaching was not Montesinos's alone but that together as a community the Dominicans had decided the issue of the treatment of the Taino needed to be addressed. Montesinos was speaking on all of their behalf. The grumbling continued, and finally at the end of the afternoon, Cordoba agreed that Montesinos would preach again the following Sunday.

A large crowd gathered the next week, expecting Montesinos to apologize. Instead, he issued an even graver warning, announcing that the Dominicans would no longer be giving absolution in the Sacrament of Penance to those who enslaved the native people of the island, effectively excommunicating a good portion of the congregation.

Livid, the island landowners wrote to King Ferdinand of Spain and followed up by sending a Franciscan priest, Alonso del Espinal, to report the "scandal" of Montesinos's judgment. The Dominicans raised monies to send Montesinos after him to argue their cause as—in the words of a contemporary— Montesinos was an "erudite man, an experienced negotiator, well-versed in dealing with difficult situations."[7] Montesinos cleverly maneuvered his way into the king's presence with a detailed report of the abuses against the Taino and managed to convert Espinal to his cause as well.

The king called together a council to look at the concern, and in 1512 the Laws of Burgos were issued, demanding an end to child labor, to compulsory work for women, and to the exploitation of laborers.[8] These laws were anemic, given the gravity of the injustice being perpetrated. They resulted in little immediate change. But they did launch a centuries-long conversation on the treatment of the indigenous peoples of the Americas.

Montesinos returned to Hispaniola in 1513. He spent the remainder of his life trying to build relations with and protect the rights of indigenous peoples. He was one of the first Dominicans to land on the southern coast of the United States, part of a failed settlement just north of Charleston, South Carolina. But most of his efforts involved the indigenous populations of Venezuela, where he was appointed by King Ferdinand to oversee the protection of native rights. Montesinos did not hesitate to use his power to confront and condemn the behavior of his fellow countrymen and continue to call for repentance. At one point, he led a frantic effort to rescue an indigenous leader and his family members after they had been kidnapped and enslaved by a well-connected Spanish official. In this, too, he failed. But he remained active for the cause. The exact year of his death is unknown, yet he is believed to have been murdered by a member of the Spanish colonial government around 1540.[9]

The Church has long struggled with the righteous use of judgment, and in particular the practice of excommunication. It is always considered a means of last resort to try to wake persons up to the gravity of their sin and elicit change of behavior. Especially in the modern world, it tends to propel persons away from the Church rather than creating a desire for repentance and reconciliation. But Montesinos understood that there are lines that cannot be crossed because they exist to protect people on the other side, and sometimes that must be stated as clearly and as strongly as possible. A grand statue of Montesinos, almost fifteen feet in height, now overlooks the Port of San Domingo in the Dominican Republic. His left hand is raised to his lips, continuing to cry out in judgment, more than five hundred years later.

For Reflection

- Reading the consequences of eating from the Tree of the Knowledge of Good and Evil is hard. How do you understand the link between eating of the tree and the consequences described? Why are these particular consequences a result of that particular choice?

- Midrash describes God creating two other worlds before our own that in the end God did not deem to be good. Why do you think it is only a world grounded on both justice and mercy that God deems pleasing?

- What associations do you have with the word *judgment* as a leader, and how do you feel when you consider that you've been entrusted with the power to judge? When you consider patterns in your leadership, do you find yourself tilting in the direction of justice or mercy?

- How does the witness of Jesus about judgment complicate or enrich your own understanding of what the power of judgment looks like when exercised righteously?

- What insight do you glean from Antonio Montesinos's story concerning the spirituality of power, especially as it relates to the challenging task of judgment?

10. Exercising the Power to Clothe

The Lord God made for the man and his wife garments of skin, with which he clothed them.

—Genesis 3:21

The discovery of the man's and woman's misdeeds begins with the sound of God walking about in the garden, and the twelfth-century Jewish rabbi Radak wanted to know why. Why did God first make a sound? Why not simply appear? "The Torah wishes to teach us something about good manners," Radak hypothesized. "God wanted to give them an opportunity to hide. One should not frighten people by addressing them suddenly without a person having had a chance to compose himself first in order to receive a visitor."[1] Not unlike a parent who realizes it is important to now knock before opening their preteen's bedroom door, God knows Adam and Eve have undergone a change. They are aware of something they had never been aware of before: their nakedness.

Nakedness is a uniquely human phenomenon, one of the features that distinguishes humans from the other creatures of the earth, and then specifically, distinguishes maturing humans from children. No other creature has a sense of shame or vulnerability appearing in its own skin. No other creature has the impulse to cover itself. But once humans have eaten from the Tree of the Knowledge of Good and Evil, this is exactly the impulse they experience, and they grasp for the best they can find in the moment—an *ezor* or loincloth made of fig leaves. It is interesting to consider that loincloths have been the first attempt humans across time and place have made at covering themselves. While peoples of different cultures and eras have clothed themselves in many different ways, almost every people in even the hottest climes have felt compelled to cover their loins. Even before clothing was necessary to buffer against cold, nakedness was a common human concern.

Throughout the ancient Near East, there existed a strong connection between covering one's body and human status. To be without clothing was a sign of not only dire poverty but also enslavement. To be without clothing meant one was entirely subject to the elements, but also often to a master. To be without clothing was to be without power. In contrast, to wear clothing was a sign of being fully human and an indication of one's likeness to the gods, who in ancient artwork were also clothed. In the Derekh Eretz Zutta—one of the minor tractates of the Talmud—it states, "Men are the glory of God and their clothes are the glory of men."[2] By observing a person's clothing, you could immediately know their status in society. Undyed wool was an indication of lower class. The whiteness of one's garment was seen as an indication of one's cleanliness, not just physically but also spiritually in terms of purity. Red was often reserved for the military and nobility, and purple was a sign of highest stature. Only a king was allowed a cloak of solid purple.[3]

It is significant then that in Genesis, before the man and woman are cast from the Garden of Eden, God insists on sewing garments and clothing them. It is an indication that God wants to protect them from the elements in this harsher new world they are entering into. It is not Eden. But it is an indication of even more. God immediately follows by stating, "See! The man has become like one of us, knowing good and evil!" (Gn 3:22). The clothing is a sign that the man and woman are distinct from the animals. It is fitting that they receive the dignity of clothing.

The Hebrew word for this garment fashioned by God is *kutonet*—a tunic of knee or ankle length. For people of biblical times, the *kutonet* was the basic undergarment everyone wore day and night, which one would then belt around the middle and cover with a cloak before going out of the home. Throughout the Hebrew Scriptures, though, the *kutonet* is frequently mentioned in association with persons of power. Joseph receives a *kutonet passim*—often translated as a "coat of many colors"—from his father Jacob. It was a sign of his belovedness (Gn 37:3). Tamar, the daughter of King David, also wears a *kutonet passim* (2 Sm 13:19). The sons of Levi, first priests of Israel, are to wear a *kutonet* as the base for all their other priestly garments (Ex 28:4).

Jesus regularly engaged the symbol of clothing in his storytelling. In his story of Lazarus at the door of the rich man, he highlights the detail of the rich man's clothing—purple atop a fine linen tunic—signifying this was a man of the highest degree of wealth (Lk 16:19). In the parable of the prodigal son who returns, the father's first impulse is to garb his wayward son: "Quickly bring the finest robe and put it on him" (Lk 15:22). In the parable of the wedding feast, however, the guest who arrives without festal attire is queried, "My friend, how is it you came in here without a wedding garment?" Unable to respond, he is tossed out of the banquet into the darkness (Mt 22:11–13). Being properly clothed was clearly serious business in Jesus's culture! It was a sign of status, dignity, and in the last case, a way of showing respect for the occasion and those with whom one has gathered.

Jesus names clothing the naked as one of the most important acts of mercy we can undertake (Mt 25:36), and while the gospels do not relay specific stories of Jesus doing this himself literally, they give examples of Jesus offering persons "cover" metaphorically. For example, after a woman is caught in adultery—a scene that suggests one caught without clothes—he chases away those who've gathered to stare at and stone her before he addresses her one-on-one (Jn 7:53–8:11).

At the end of Jesus's life, the gospels make note of Jesus being stripped of his garments and mocked by soldiers who wrap him in a red or purple cloak as he is beaten. John's gospel makes special note of Jesus's personal cloak being divided into four pieces at the foot of the Cross, but his tunic—because it was seamless—was raffled off at the roll of dice. The scene reminds us that crucifixion was not only physically excruciating but also humiliating—an indication that one was considered an animal. At the same time, the scene subtly draws attention to Jesus's inviolable status; the only other garment described as seamless in the contemporary literature is Josephus's description of the tunic of the Temple high priest.[4]

In Baptism, each of us has received a white garment, evoking memories of biblical garments from the beginning of time, reminding us of our dignity—indeed, our royal and priestly status. We are told within the rite to keep it "unstained into the everlasting life of heaven." In so many ways, we might think of that garment as the basic dress code for Christian leadership. Whatever other vesture linked to our role that we put on each day—the suit coat, the chasuble, the scrubs, the silk scarf, or the veil—it goes atop the *kutonet* given to us by our heavenly Father.

As those granted inviolable dignity, we are called to share in God's act of clothing others. Sometimes this power to clothe can be understood quite literally: clothing our children, clothing refugees, or clothing the patient in the hospital bed. But like Jesus, in leadership, we are probably more often called upon to clothe others metaphorically—in the way we deal with those who have been exposed in some way and our communications on sensitive concerns. Physical clothing is more readily available than ever before in history, but the sense of being exposed or naked is still very much part of the human experience.

We live in a time of twenty-four-hour news cycles where the hunger for information is voracious and transparency is demanded while pleas for privacy are regarded as suspect. There is good reason for people to want the truth. Too often information that has been critical for our health and well-being has been withheld from us—for example, by corporations trying to cover up information about chemical spills or the tobacco industry trying to hide the effects of cigarettes.

At the same time, our desire for information goes far beyond what is necessary for our own well-being of mind, body, and spirit. It involves what Augustine of Hippo and Thomas Aquinas would call *curiositas*,[5] the lurid fascination with the personal woes of celebrities and public figures—who broke up with whom, who gained fifty pounds, or who was arrested for a DUI. We revel in the exposé. Aquinas argued the importance of truthfulness but also noted there are limits to this virtue. Whatever news is reported must be true, but not all that is true needs to be reported. The truth is owed only to those who need to know, either for their own health and well-being or to fulfill their designated role in society.[6] So, does one's doctor need to know about a drug overdose? Yes. Does the nation at large need to know? Probably not.

As leaders, by virtue of the roles we occupy, we often hold sensitive information about others' lives that could make them feel naked or ashamed or exposed. We have the power to "dress down" someone or the power to offer them "cover." Sometimes the information we hold is revealed freely to us in spiritual direction or confession. More often it comes to us from a required employment background check, a complaint filed by a coworker, or gossip overheard in the parking lot. Our filing cabinets and computers hold others' performance reviews, transcripts, and psychological assessments. We have the key to the congregational archives or sacramental records where family information is recorded. By honoring the confidentiality appropriate to our role, every day we protect others' human dignity.[7]

As many leaders know, however, the right use of this "power over" others that we possess by virtue of having their sensitive information can present a dilemma: what may be shameful to one person may be information another would find important to have for their well-being. The Catholic Church's sexual abuse crisis is an example of how multiple bishops, in offering cover to their priests—often out of the desire to spare them shame—then made it possible for some of these same priests to continue abusing children and teens in new settings. Important information was cloaked when it should have been exposed, even if it meant the priest ended up on the front page of the news.

Many situations, though, are not so clear cut. "When I discovered one of our faculty members had had an inappropriately intimate relationship with one of our graduate students, I knew I needed to let him go," relayed a former head of a school. "There was no evidence this had ever happened before and he was deeply repentant. I saw no need for the whole school to know. He left under the guise of having a family member who needed care." Would the former head feel differently about the decision if news of other inappropriate relationships had later emerged? "Oh, definitely," came the reply.

The skill the Church expects leaders to exercise in these situations is discretion. "No governmental system in history has been without significant discretionary power; none can be," reads a US Conference of Catholic Bishops document on resolving conflicts. "Discretion is indispensable for tailoring decisions to unique facts and circumstances in particular cases and for creative solutions to new problems. Total elimination of discretionary power would cripple authority's service to the people by depriving that service of all flexibility." At the same time, the document acknowledges how easily discretion can end up going awry: "The conceded need for necessary discretionary power in Church administrators, however, must not be allowed to becloud one's vision of the large opportunities for abuse of such powers."[8] Discretion, for better or worse, is more an art than a science. Whether we made the right or wrong judgment will often not be confirmed until many years later.

In interviews, several leaders mentioned the distinction they make between their public duty and their private care. "We have a man in our community who needed to be removed from ministry for accusations of inappropriate conduct from decades ago," relayed a brother from a religious order: "He is in a nursing home now. I will never condone abuse, and at the same time, I will visit him in the nursing home every time I am in town. I don't stop caring about him as a person because of what he has done. He is still one of my brothers, and his human needs—including for companionship—still need to be met."

"I had a priest who was assigned by his bishop to the hospital as a chaplain," added a vice president of mission in health care:

> He was unhappy about it and it showed in his work. Multiple times I had to write him up for not answering his phone when he was on call, and it went into his employment file. Soon I was going to have to fire him, but it wasn't that I didn't care

about him and his future. I worked to help get him
a scholarship to go back to school so that he'd have
other options available—so that he could have a
dignified "out."

Once upon a time, scripture tells us the first man and
woman awakened to their nakedness and the world
became a harsher, less hospitable place. While God did
not turn back time for them, God also did not send
them out into this new world exposed. We who've
known the experience of shame and vulnerability
in our own lives understand just how tender God's
gesture was. It moves us to want to exercise our power
in similarly tender ways. Because the power to clothe is
one exercised when others are feeling at their worst, it
requires us to show up at our best: continuing to love
people even when we hate their actions, continuing
to preserve their human dignity even as we resist
enabling bad behavior to continue, and offering a
kutonet because, no matter what they have done, they
will always be God's beloved.

Companion for the Journey: **Hildegard of Bingen**

Hildegard, like every teen of every age, had some
information that she did not want publicly known:
since the age of three she had been experiencing
vivid, colorful visions. Her parents knew of course.
This may have been one of the main reasons they

decided to entrust her at a young age to the Benedictine monastery in Disibodenberg, Germany. Jutta also knew. Jutta was the noblewoman, only a couple of years older than Hildegard, to whom she was specifically entrusted and with whom she lived in close quarters until Jutta's death when Hildegard was thirty-eight. And Volmar knew. Volmar was the Benedictine priest assigned to care for Jutta and Hildegard. But neither Jutta nor Volmar made much fuss about these visions, and Hildegard did not want to either.

The visions were odd. They were also potentially dangerous: What if they drew the attention of Church officials? What if they were considered evil or erroneous? In recent decades, scientists have wondered whether Hildegard's visions might have been a case of scintillating scotomata—not unheard of among chronic migraine sufferers. Throughout her life, Hildegard experienced periods of pain where she was unable to get out of bed for days on end. But whatever the source, Hildegard and those who cared for her kept these visions quiet until, at the age of forty-two, she had a vision unlike any she had experienced before:

"And it came to pass," she writes, "in the eleven hundred and forty-first year of the incarnation of Jesus Christ . . . that the heavens were opened and a blinding light of exceptional brilliance flowed through my entire brain. And so it kindled my whole heart and breast like a flame, . . . and suddenly I understood the meaning of the [scriptures]."[9] Hildegard heard the command to

record her visions and share them with others. She was
hesitant. Again, others might label them as insanity or
heresy rather than divine revelation, but she now felt
compelled to make public what she had hidden for
so long. Over the course of ten years, with Volmar's
assistance, she described and helped to artistically
capture twenty-six visions in a book titled *Know the
Ways of the Lord* (commonly called *Scivias*). This book
was followed by two other religious tomes: *The Book
of Life's Merits*, about the life of virtue, and *The Book of
Divine Works*, about salvation history.

Themes from the first three chapters of Genesis
feature prominently across Hildegard's writings,
including the theme of clothing. Hildegard envisioned
creation as God's clothing, the visible garment of an
invisible divinity. Creation vibrated with the energy of
life, or what she referred to as *viriditas*, greenness. The
plant world, in particular, provided humans with the
nourishment and healing needed to thrive. In addition
to her religious books, Hildegard wrote two books on
the natural world and on medicine, demonstrating her
extensive knowledge of local flora and fauna.

It was not only God who was clothed in Hildegard's
visions though. After the Fall, she envisioned God—in
the form of Wisdom—clothing humans: "In her secret
zeal, she has sought gentleness like wool and piety
like linen. . . . She has protected the sons of men lest
they walk naked before God."[10] Hildegard imagined
different virtues as different colors of clothing with love

represented by a constantly changing color, as love has so many different manifestations.

Hildegard's visions, rather than being condemned, drew many—including Church officials—to seek her counsel. Hildegard founded and served as the abbess of two women's monasteries in Bingen and Rüdesheim, along the Rhine River. People far and near sought her out for healing or a word from the Lord. She carried on extensive correspondence with bishops, abbots, nobles, and even the Holy Roman Emperor Frederick Barbarossa. She mediated disputes in other monasteries. She conducted four preaching tours throughout Germany. In her spare time, Hildegard wrote more than seventy songs and created her own language of nine hundred words for her sisters to use.

As the years went on, Hildegard grew less hesitant to claim the insights and knowledge with which she was gifted. Her speech became bolder; her advice, more frank. She was especially outspoken on behalf of the reforms instituted by Pope Gregory VII trying to right abuses of power within the Church. Hildegard fearlessly confronted Barbarossa on his resistance to these reforms. "I see you like a little boy or some madman," she wrote. "The blindness of your eyes . . . fail to see correctly how to hold the rod of proper governance in your hand."[11] Likewise, she did not hesitate to dress down clerics for their laxity, especially regarding sexual mores.

The loss of Volmar in 1173 was a source of great grief for Hildegard. He had served as her scribe and friend for over sixty years at this point, and for the remainder of her life she struggled to find another companion like him. Five years later, her lack of an advocate among the local clergy became problematic when Hildegard allowed a man to be buried in the monastery cemetery who had previously been excommunicated. Hildegard knew that the man had made a confession before he died and believed him to be reconciled with the Church. She wanted to clothe him with the dignity of a Christian burial. The clergy of nearby Mainz, however, wanted his body disinterred and removed from Church property. Hildegard refused. She blessed the grave and then removed any indication of where he was buried so his grave could not be disturbed. Some versions of the story have Hildegard's sisters removing all of the headstones in the graveyard. The monastery was put under interdict, and the sisters were not allowed to sing the Divine Office, only whisper the words.

Now eighty years old, however, Hildegard was done with whispering and refused to be denied singing her own music. She drew upon her extensive network of Church connections and the power of her own voice to write letters, garner evidence supporting her case, and have the judgment against her monastery removed. In the end, the archbishop of Mainz requested *her* forgiveness. She died six months later in September

1179. "Just as someone puts on a cloth woven from threads and wears it," Hildegard had written, "the soul, put[s] on . . . works—whether good or ill—as a garment and is covered with the deeds that it performed."[12] Hildegard wove the final thread of her garment in protecting the dignity of another.

For Reflection

- Do you remember at what age you first felt aware of your "nakedness" and the desire to "cover yourself"? How was that need respected by the adults in your life? If it was not respected, what effect do you think that had on you?

- Have you associated clothing as a sign of human dignity before? Do you think that clothing has the same meaning in our own culture as in biblical times? Is clothing still a sign of status?

- Besides bodily privacy, are there other things you think people should have a right to keep private? As a leader, how do you try to help others' privacy to be respected?

- Can you think of a time when someone in power (a parent, teacher, boss, etc.) "clothed" you when you were feeling "exposed"? What did you learn from this experience?

- What guidelines do you have for yourself as a leader about when to share what might be another's shameful information and when to keep it confidential, acknowledging there can be abuses of power in both directions?

- What do you glean from the life of St. Hildegard of Bingen about what it means to live the power to clothe in a healthy and holy way?

11. Exercising the Power to Start Anew

> The man had intercourse with his wife Eve, and she conceived and gave birth to Cain, saying, "I have produced a male child with the help of the LORD."
>
> —Genesis 4:1

Chapter 3 of Genesis closes with Adam and Eve being driven from the Garden of Eden with "the cherubim and the fiery ever-turning sword" stationed "to guard the way to the tree of life" (Gn 3:24). It seems like the story is over before it has barely begun. Henceforth humans are condemned to drudgery, haunted forever by regret. They will never have access to the Tree of Life again. Or will they?

If you've made it to chapter 11 in this book, you know that there is always more than one way to interpret a passage. What if, asks the nineteenth-century German rabbi Samson Raphael Hirsch, the cherubim and sword are stationed "to guard the way to the tree of life" to ensure "that a way remains open"? What if now life is about journeying on that way—learning from the trials of the world (the sword) on one side of the road and God's revealed truth (the cherubim) on the other side?[1] What if this exit from the garden *isn't* the end of the story of creation but a new start?

Chapter 4 of Genesis begins on a hopeful note. The man "knew his wife Eve"—again the Hebrew word *da'* suggesting intimate or sexual knowledge—and Eve gives birth to Cain (*qa-yin*). The name is a play on the Hebrew phrase for "I have gained" or "I have produced" (*qa-ni-ti*). The statement Eve makes upon Cain's birth is interesting as it carries echoes of her own creation story. In Genesis 2:23, God creates the woman (*ishah*) by taking her from the side of the man (*ish*), but now in Genesis 4:1, the woman produces a man (*ish*) from *her* body. The Hebrew word suggests a grown adult rather than a child. Still, the message is clear: human beings may not be immortal, but they will still go on via their capacity to produce new generations.

Eve knows that in bearing a son she has participated in God's own creative power—a fact she makes explicit when she adds to her statement "*YHWH 'et.*" But the intended message here is not so clear. The phrase is often translated as "with the help of the LORD." However, it could also be that Eve is comparing herself to God, as in "I have brought life into the world as did our LORD." So perhaps she is grateful. Or perhaps she is prideful. Perhaps she is simply coming into contact with her own power. All of these are possibilities—as they are for us when we discover within ourselves the power to get up after a fall, dust ourselves off, and begin to exercise power anew.

The power to start anew is one of the divine powers highlighted throughout scripture. In many ways, the whole of the Bible is a story of God's relentless tenacity in the face of challenges and disappointments. We've hinted before at some of God's challenges and disappointments that find their way into the creation stories: God separates the waters, but sometimes the waters still leak through. God creates animals, but none is found a suitable partner for *adam*. God fashions an idyllic setting for the first humans, but they violate its rules. What perhaps we should make more explicit as we draw toward the end of this book is that no challenge or disappointment ever makes God give up on the project of creation, and on humanity in particular. For God, there is always a tomorrow—another opportunity to try out a new approach.

That enduring hope, that capacity for resiliency—so difficult to distinguish from stubborn pride—is a gift that God has shared with us. When Eve says "YHWH 'et," she speaks for all of us who are still standing, still trying, and still in the game, by the grace of God working within us. "How old were you when you came into this sense of agency you have?" I asked a school administrator who always impresses me with her grit. She laughed aloud. "Today years old!" she replied. "That's like asking someone when they were saved. It's not a onetime thing. It's something that has to happen anew for me every day."

The most seasoned leaders are generally where they are because they have an abundance of this power to rebound. They are where they are because they are not easily discouraged. But it does not mean that they have not *faced* discouragement or do not *continue* to have discouraging experiences. Even "the powerful" have experiences of being unable to exercise their will and effect changes they want to see. Even "the powerful" have experiences of feeling helpless, ashamed, regretful, and punched in the gut. But whether these experiences will take one toward the Tree of Life or away from it has to do with how these things are processed along the way.

Throughout the past ten chapters, we've named some of the behaviors associated with people experiencing power: They are more comfortable speaking up and asking questions. They take up more physical space and more space in the conversation. They are more optimistic, more sure of their perspective, more willing to take risks, and more generous. They are comfortable initiating contact. We've talked about these behaviors as a mixed bag. In general, they are neutral—perhaps even good—qualities, yet they can go in dangerous directions and have unintended impacts.

The same is actually true of behaviors associated with people experiencing powerlessness. People experiencing powerlessness often maintain a large gap between what they think and what they will say. When they do speak, they are more likely to use "mitigated speech"—speaking in the form of suggestions or hints, but not straightforwardly saying what they mean. They are more likely to exhibit passive-aggressive behaviors, triangulation, and misplaced anger (since they often are unable to express anger directly toward those "in power"). They are more pessimistic, more self-doubting, and more cautious. They are less likely to initiate contact and hold what they have tightly, as it could all be taken away.

These behaviors, too, are a mixed bag. It is not as if the behaviors of those with power are evil and the behaviors of those without power are virtuous. Rather, reflecting health and holiness for those who experience themselves as powerless requires courageously integrating more behaviors associated with power into their lives. And reflecting health and holiness for those who *do* have power requires integrating and learning from their ongoing experiences of powerlessness in positive ways.

Note that these two categories—being powerful and feeling powerless—are not mutually exclusive. It is possible to not have much authority in the workplace or be a member of an underprivileged group and still experience a lot of power internally. It is also possible to have a position of great authority or be part of a privileged class in society and still not experience oneself as powerful. The worst abuses of power are committed by those who objectively speaking hold a great deal of power: they have important positions and hold a lot of sway over others, but they don't see it or don't feel it. They continue to see themselves as a victim—oppressed, voiceless, and inconsequential— even when in reality their actions greatly affect others. They exhibit behaviors associated with powerlessness that are, at best, unhelpful and, at worst, cause significant harm.

For those of us who have power and acknowledge it—those of us reading this book—I want to reiterate a point from the introduction: the spiritual and moral task does not involve abdicating our power. As self-help author Marianne Williamson has famously written, "We ask ourselves, Who am I to be brilliant, gorgeous, talented, fabulous? Actually, who are you *not* to be? You are a child of God. Your playing small doesn't serve the world."[2] The spiritual and moral task instead involves learning how to deal with ongoing experiences of powerlessness in healthy rather than aberrant ways—ways that build resilience, not weaken it.

But how? When humbled by life, how does one bounce back rather than become mired in a sense of victimhood? This was one of the questions I pursued most tenaciously in the interviews that led to this book, with two significant themes emerging.

First, resilient leaders live the strange paradox of knowing themselves to be both great and small, mighty and weak at the same time. They know their actions are consequential while also knowing the universe does not revolve around them. They know they have authority while also knowing they are not the Messiah. They often frame this awareness in the context of a bigger plan existing, in which they play a little part. A director of school accreditation shared, "What keeps me faithful and honest is that I'm doing my part in this little hiccup in history. I will be but a comma in time, even if I live to be ninety."

"What keeps me going is that I look at this as a long story," stated a pastor.

> There are lots of things that are beyond my comprehension at this moment. I have appreciated the wisdom of brother priests who have been pastors longer. There have been situations where I thought I was powerless, but there was still some little thing I could do that would be helpful, and they've helped me to see that. And when there really was nothing I could do, they've taught me it is a moment to pray and realize there is a bigger picture and I can't see it all. None of us knows how it'll all shake out.

Second, when resilient leaders experience powerlessness, as unpleasant as that experience is, they choose to view it as part of the way *to* the Tree of Life rather than something blocking its access. In essence, they choose to name it as an opportunity for solidarity or learning. While not having things go as we want never feels good, it remains an important experience to have occasionally because it is the experience many people have *every day*. Such experiences remind us how life looks from the vantage point of those who spend a lot more time in powerlessness than we do, and can help us have more empathy.

Moreover, remember those enduring, stable sources of power that we talked about at the end of chapter 7—integrity and authenticity? The ones that truly keep us grounded as holy and healthy leaders? Unfortunately, they never come to us on a silver platter. Other sources of power, such as social class, job title, or fame, can be acquired by accident of birth or luck. But as one vice president in healthcare told me, "I call them floaties. They will keep you from drowning only for a bit until you can prove your character and build relationships." The character-based sources of power, such as integrity and authenticity, are forged in the crucible of challenge and disappointment. For better or worse, there is no other way to acquire them except through personal experiences of wrestling with powerlessness.[3]

Aware of the harsh reality that experiences of powerlessness are an important counterbalance to experiences of power, the healthiest leaders actually *seek* opportunities where they will not be in charge or be the expert in the field. They do so to not lose contact with what it is like to be powerless and to forge character. "If I catch myself trying to flex my power, then I have stepped out from under the shadow of the Cross and need to get back under it," a popular speaker and online church planter told me. "I try to keep a rhythm of not being in a powerful place too much. I will not be on the stage on back-to-back days. I need to step to the back of the auditorium and do other things so that I remember to come under the one who truly has authority."

Her comments hint at a practice leadership coach Julie Diamond names as "cultivating role conflict."[4] In order to be a healthier leader, Diamond advocates, always have at least one setting in your life in which you are *not* the leader or—better yet—not even remotely competent. It should be a space where you are learning something new, where you are not special. You might volunteer in a ministry you know little about, travel to a country where you do not know the language, or get mentored in a new craft. Putting yourself in situations where you are not the leader reorients you to reality and teaches you to welcome new beginnings rather than fear them. "Good leaders," Diamond says, "learn how to 'be nobody' in the midst of being somebody."[5]

Perhaps the best example we have of the "cultivating role conflict" practice in action is the Incarnation. Talk about a "Somebody" learning to be a nobody! Jesus is the God who had to learn to walk, the Wisdom of All Ages who had to learn how to speak. "I take the greatest consolation," a bishop relayed to me, "in the line from Hebrews: 'He is able to deal patiently with the ignorant and erring, for he himself is beset by weakness'" (Heb 5:2).

For all the power that Jesus exhibited in his convening and blessing, questioning and judging, and so forth, we can easily imagine there were also times when Jesus felt powerless. Perhaps we can sense the frustration in his voice when his disciples continued not to grasp his teaching. Or we can hear his mounting volume when arguing with the Pharisees and Sadducees. We can remember the day he cursed the fig tree. These are all typical behaviors of one who is not able to have what he wants to see happen actually happen. Perhaps these experiences are what also forged in Jesus his sense of compassion for those on the margins of society who rarely "get their way" and a resiliency so strong that even death could not steal his tomorrow.

With the help of God, Eve dusted herself off after losing her immortality in the garden and became immortal in another way through giving birth to a new generation. The debacle with the snake and the casting from Eden was not the end of her story after all. It was the beginning of ours. As Eve's descendants, perhaps there is no power we can exercise that delights God more than when we overcome fear and discouragement and exercise the power to get up, bounce back, and start anew. It certainly is the power that we have *needed* to exercise most in human history. But it is likely also the one that gives God the greatest joy because it communicates that we, too, have not given up on the project of creation, and on the great human experiment in particular. We, too, have hope for the future. And as Christians, we can acknowledge that the way of the Cross Jesus revealed to us and the way to the Tree of Life Genesis lifts up, in the end, are one and the same journey: eternal life is found by passing *through* the trials of the world, illumined by truth, not around them.

Companion for the Journey: **Mark Ji Tianxiang**

There are saints who look lovely on holy cards— youthful and attractive, while holding bouquets of lilies. St. Mark Ji Tianxiang is not one of those saints. With his skeletal frame and hollowed-out eyes, while holding an opium pipe in his open hand, images of Tianxiang are sure to shock. Who is *this* man, and why is *he* a saint?

Mark Ji Tianxiang was born in 1834 to a Christian family in the Jizhou district of Hebei, about two hundred miles south of Beijing, China. While little is known of his own childhood, much has been written of the time in which he grew up. The Qing dynasty was entering a season of long decline, making it vulnerable to the interests of Western countries wanting access to Chinese tea, silk, and porcelain. Finding these products costly to purchase in silver, the English began to trade for them in opium from India.

Following the "Opium Wars" of 1839–1842 and 1856–1860, the English, and then other Western nations, wrested concession after concession from the Chinese government, opening up more ports for trade and flooding the country with the popular painkiller and recreational drug. Chinese officials, eager to stem the resulting trade imbalance, encouraged the local growth of opium, further increasing its use even as its dangers were becoming more widely known. By the turn of the century, approximately 27 percent of adult men in the country were addicted to opium—a degree of mass addiction unequaled in any nation before or since.[6] "We can tell them at once," wrote a missionary to China in the late 1800s, "by their deathly faces and black teeth."[7]

Tianxiang married and became a physician in Jizhou, likely around the time of the Second Opium War. As a physician, he held a highly respected role in his community—a respect further elevated by his reputation for generosity, treating those without money for free. In his mid-thirties, however, Tianxiang himself contracted a serious stomach ailment and managed his own pain by taking opium. At the time, the drug was regarded as especially effective against digestive troubles, so it was not unusual for a doctor to prescribe. But like many, Tianxiang found that once he started taking the drug, it was not easy to stop.

As a Catholic, Tianxiang sought help in the Sacrament of Penance, seeking forgiveness and the grace to conquer his addiction. Indeed, he pursued confession so regularly that finally the priest told him to stop coming. In the late 1800s, there was little understanding of how addiction functioned. The priest viewed Tianxiang's opium use as a sin and forbade him from receiving Eucharist until he could free himself of the drug. Every day Tianxiang awoke intending to begin anew, and every day Tianxiang found himself unable to stop. But he never gave up trying. Remarkably, Tianxiang continued to attend Eucharist without receiving for over thirty years, even as he suffered the scorn of his faith community for being a "junkie."

In 1899, when Tianxiang was sixty-five years old, the Yihetuan Movement—also known as the Boxer Rebellion—broke out in the nearby province of Shandong. Led by young nationalists skilled in martial arts (hence the label "Boxers"), the movement initially sought to quell a rise of crime in the region but quickly took on anti-imperialist overtones. Christians became part of the Yihetuan's target since Christian missionaries were seen as allied with the European nations whose trade practices had decimated the country—sometimes even arriving on the same ships carrying the opium. Furthermore, the missionaries occasionally harbored the thieves responsible for the crime wave when these thieves identified as

Christian converts. The Yihetuan spread through the northeastern China countryside, including the Tianxiang's Hebei Province, burning down churches and killing Christians as it moved toward Beijing, where many of the European government and trade representatives lived.

The conflict climaxed in the early summer of 1900, as the Yihetuan laid siege on the area of Beijing populated by the European legates. The Empress Dowager Cixi took the Yihetuan's side, declaring war on all foreign powers present in China. Chinese Christians far and wide were rounded up as foreign sympathizers and told to renounce their faith or face death. In all, thirty-two thousand Chinese Christians— Protestant, Catholic, and Orthodox—were killed, as well as two hundred European and American missionaries.

Among those arrested that violent summer were Tianxiang, his son, two daughters-in-law, and six grandchildren. At his trial, Tianxiang was given the chance to abandon his Christian belief and be spared, but he refused and encouraged his family members to do likewise. Instead, Tianxiang begged for the "privilege" of being put to death last so that none of his family members would die alone. He and his family were put to death on July 7, 1900.

The story of Mark Ji Tianxiang is a messy one. At the time of his death, Tianxiang was still experiencing powerlessness in his battle with opium and still without the strength so many of us derive from participating in the sacraments. Yet in his thirty-year effort to overcome addiction, Tianxiang had developed the capacity to look fear and immense suffering in the eye and remain undeterred. On his last day, he found he had all the strength anyone could ask for, well prepared for God's tomorrow.

For Reflection

- When have you, like Eve, experienced a significant setback or failure and been able to exercise the power to start anew?

- What are the lessons that experiences of power-lessness have taught you? How do you try to incorporate these lessons into your practice of leadership now?

- What do you make of the assertion that the worst abuses of power are actually committed by persons who have power but feel powerless? What helps to keep you from exhibiting behaviors associated with powerlessness when you are feeling discouraged?

- Do you ever intentionally put yourself into situations where you are not the leader, where you feel like a beginner again? What would keep you from doing so?

- What insight do you glean from Mark Ji Tianxiang's story concerning the spirituality of power, especially as it relates to resilience?

12. On Laying Down One's Power

> On the seventh day God completed the work he had been doing; he rested on the seventh day from all the work he had undertaken. God blessed the seventh day and made it holy, because on it he rested from all the work he had done in creation.
>
> —Genesis 2:2–3

It is an odd thing, notes twentieth-century rabbi Abraham Heschel, that Genesis 2:1 speaks of God finishing the work of creation on the seventh day. Wasn't God's work of creation finished at the end of day six? Day six was the day humans were created. It is the day God pronounced not just "good" but "very good." But no, Heschel reminds us, humans are not the crown jewel of the process of creation. That honor belongs to *menuha*. The word is often translated from Hebrew into English as "rest," but Heschel laments this anemic choice of terms. *Menuha* means so much more than relaxation or inactivity. *Menuha* means tranquility, wholeness, and peace. It is the "end" of creation.[1]

To call *menuha* the "end" of creation can easily be misunderstood. It does not mean that God's creation has come to a close, that nothing new will happen in time. And it certainly doesn't mean that God is done interacting with the world. Using the image of a pencil, one could say that the "end" of a pencil is the eraser. But one could also say that the "end" of the pencil is the point. The "end" of the pencil is to write. So, to say *menuha* is the "end" of creation means that all of creation is pointed in the direction of tranquility, wholeness, and peace. *Menuha* is the purpose for which time was created, and for which history exists.

As many scripture scholars have observed, the other days of creation are named as good, but the seventh day is the only one named as *qadosh*, holy. Indeed, this is the first time the word *qadosh* appears in all of scripture. The first thing that God sanctifies and sets apart is not an object—a thing in space—but rather a day—an event in time.

The ancient Jewish practice of Sabbath—known within the Jewish community as Shabbat—seeks to honor the holiness of the seventh day by truly setting it apart from the rest of the week. While the practice is rooted in the first creation story of Genesis, the expectations related to it are described more fully elsewhere in the Bible, particularly in the book of Exodus. Shabbat involves the cessation of all forms of productive activity—any sort of activity that would change one's environment—from sunset on Friday evening (the beginning of the biblical seventh day) till sunset on Saturday evening.

In lieu of work, one is to spend the day as humans might in the Garden of Eden—visiting with friends and family, lingering at the table enjoying previously prepared meals, napping, engaging in sex for married couples, singing, studying the scripture, and participating in worship. Just as Jesus convened at table with many different sorts of people as a way of practicing the reign of God into being (see chapter 4), Shabbat practices the seventh day into being. It is a reminder each week of the kind of life God dreams for us, the "end" of creation that we have not yet seen but long for. It is a way of bringing the future into the present and delighting in it.[2]

Who wouldn't want to spend time like this once a week? Who wouldn't want to spend a whole day resting from labor and enjoying a taste of *menuha*—joining God in a long, loving gaze upon the world and savoring the beauty of it all? Well, apparently, most of us. Although honoring the Sabbath is one of the Ten Commandments, which we consider foundational for living a moral life, most of us seem to treat it as a nice suggestion. The practice of Shabbat sounds delightful, which should make it the most attractive commandment to follow, but instead we find it the hardest. And why is this? Heschel suspects it has something to do with power and the mystery of time.

Heschel notes that as human beings, we spend a great deal of our week dealing with the things of space. To return to the most basic definition of power from the beginning of this book, power is the ability to change something in space. Be it through the physical labor of our hands, our words, the act of convening a group, or any of the other powers named in this book, power is about making the world into a different sort of place than it currently is. We clear fields and harvest crops, establish governments, do business, educate youth, and treat the sick. And six days a week, Heschel says, to work in this arena of space is good and right. It is our human vocation to collaborate with God in the ongoing transformation of the earth, to exercise dominion. But there is one power God has elected *not* to share with us. "The power we attain in the world of space terminates abruptly at the borderline of time," Heschel says.[3] No matter how we might like to add or subtract hours of the day, or months of the year, we are all powerless before this fact: time continues to belong only to God.

To admit that there is one dimension of reality in which we do not exercise dominion is difficult—for some of us impossibly so. We fight against it daily. Our inability to control time and bend it to our will as we can with space is a constant source of frustration, and even terror as the years of our lives slip between our fingers like sand and there is not a thing we can do to stop it. "Time to us is a sarcasm," states Heschel, "a slick treacherous monster with a jaw like a furnace incinerating every moment of our lives. Shrinking, therefore, from facing time, we escape for shelter to things of space. . . . But things of space are not fireproof; they only add fuel to the flames. . . . The more we think, the more we realize: we cannot conquer time through space. We can only master time in time."[4]

In this sense, yes, honoring the Sabbath each week sounds lovely, but it requires tremendous self-discipline. It forces us to let go of our dominion for a day and not only accept but also embrace—indeed celebrate—powerlessness. Says Heschel, "He who wants to enter the holiness of the day must first lay down the profanity of clattering commerce, of being yoked to toil. . . . He must say farewell to manual work and learn to understand that the world has already been created and will survive without the help of man."[5] What? The world needs me but also *doesn't* need me? It needs this task done urgently, but *not* today? My work is important, but also *not* important? Yes. Each week Sabbath orients us to a greater reality: Six days a week, we are to embrace the human vocation to be God's representative on earth and do that in a healthy and holy way. But one day a week, we must remember that we are not God and that this whole Project Earth Experiment is in hands bigger than our own. It's disorienting, but we do our best to live into the mystery—even as we know there are emails to be answered and a report still to be done and a fix-it project waiting in the basement.

To be frank, part of the challenge Christians face in trying to honor the Sabbath has to do with Jesus. The gospels give few hints as to the role Shabbat played in Jesus's life, and the few hints that we do glean seem to suggest that he had the practice of dismissing it: We have a couple of examples of Jesus healing on Shabbat and a pithy line attributed to him in Mark 2:27: "The sabbath was made for man, not man for the sabbath." Jesus, though, would have seen these healings as parables of the Sabbath—in essence, a reflection of the wholeness Shabbat envisions, rather than "work." And the line from Mark is actually a phrase the Pharisees would have already known within their own tradition: "The Sabbath is given unto you, not you unto the Sabbath."[6] Jesus did not come up with this notion himself. Judaism, too, puts a higher priority on saving a life than on Sabbath laws. As Christians, though, we tend to use these examples to show it is okay to do any sort of work on the Sabbath if there is a felt need.

The matter is further complicated by the line that follows: "That is why the Son of Man is lord even of the sabbath" (Mk 2:28). This verse has been the source of much reflection in the life of the Church. The gospels tell us that Jesus himself died on the sixth day of the week and that he observed Shabbat in the tomb before rising, an event that took place not on the seventh day of the week but on the first—the day that light was created. Sometimes in the history of Christianity, we will also hear the day of the Resurrection honored as the "eighth day," the day that broke out of the seven-day cycle and began a whole new era of history. Whereas in Judaism, Shabbat is a name for God—in the sense that God is our final "end," our great peace, and our final wholeness—in Christianity, Sabbath has become associated with Jesus, the Lord of the Sabbath. Jesus is the "end" of history, the one who embodies peace and wholeness, the one who has ushered in the eternal Shabbat. "For us the true Sabbath is the person of our Redeemer, our Lord Jesus Christ," claimed the sixth-century church father Gregory the Great.[7]

The earliest Christians would have both observed the Jewish Shabbat on Saturday each week and then gathered for Eucharist at the end of Shabbat, the beginning of Sunday. But over time, the difficulties of honoring both the seventh and first days of the week meant that one day began to take prominence over the other. Pope John Paul II acknowledges this in his 1998 apostolic letter *Dies Domini* (*The Day of the Lord*).[8] On one hand, as Christians, it is fitting that our week revolves around the day of the Resurrection of Christ. And from that lens, it is fitting to refer to Sunday now as the Christian Sabbath. But as John Paul II points out, Sunday has a celebratory character, and it can be hard to hold together notions of resting and celebrating in one day (*Dies Domini*, 23–27). The resting part tends to be consistently put on the back burner. Among Western Christians at least, I think it is fair to say that not only do we consider "Keeping holy the Sabbath" the most dispensable of the Ten Commandments but also we wouldn't know how to keep it holy if we wanted to. Our imagination of what Sabbath rest might even look like is impoverished.

Yet rest remains a fundamental human need. "The alternation between work and rest, built into human nature, is willed by God himself," John Paul II states:

> Rest is something "sacred," because it is man's way of withdrawing from the sometimes excessively demanding cycle of earthly tasks in order to renew his awareness that everything is the work of God. There is a risk that the prodigious power over creation which God gives to man can lead him to forget that God is the Creator upon whom everything depends. (*Dies Domini*, 65)

He urges Christians to recover a genuine commitment to rest, not just for themselves, but also for others— most especially those who work in the lower-paying service industries who are most in danger of not enjoying a day of rest. The biblical commandment on Sabbath was never meant for just the people of Israel; rather, it was meant for anyone who works for them, their animals, and even foreigners residing in their towns (see Ex 20:8–11).

As leaders, we have a special duty to pay attention to these words. As with every power described in this book, our choice to cease exercising power on Sabbath *or not* has heightened impact. We often think that denying ourselves Sabbath rest is a decision that affects only ourselves. If we want to work a little more to catch up, others should be grateful that we'd sacrifice our Sunday afternoon to answer their emails. It's noble. But in reality, if we refuse to honor our own need for rest, we are more likely not to honor others' need for rest. We are more likely to make it difficult for them to honor Sabbath as well. As John Paul II states,

> In our own historical context there remains the obligation to ensure that everyone can enjoy the freedom, rest and relaxation which human dignity requires, together with the associated religious, family, cultural and interpersonal needs which are difficult to meet if there is no guarantee of at least one day of the week on which people can *both* rest and celebrate. (*Dies Domini*, 66)

Because so many of us who are in leadership got where we are by working very long hours, it may be more difficult for us than for others to stop working. As soon as we try, we will face all of our own internal demons: We will feel antsy and distracted, as if we are wasting time. We will even feel guilty and selfish. "To take Sabbath seriously would require me to say no to some things," admitted a health care leader. "I'm a people pleaser, and it is hard to do something that would make someone not happy with me." "I like a good agenda," relayed a catechetical leader, "and practicing Sabbath requires me to make space

for attending to the Spirit's movement within myself
without having an agenda." We may need the help of
others to get started. A school superintendent told me,

> One day a month I go to one of our schools that
> has a small room next to the chapel that they set
> aside for me. I pray and take a nap. They feed me.
> It is so grounding, and my spirit feels renewed.
> I never would have thought this was such an
> important part of leadership, but I've only been
> able to maintain this practice because I have a very
> firm administrative assistant who religiously holds
> that time on my calendar for me.

Ultimately, we will be able to exercise power in
holy and healthy ways only if we are also able to cease
exercising power. Why? It sounds strange to say, but
beyond our physical need for rest, and even beyond our
spiritual need to battle whatever demons keep us from
resting, Sabbath is a necessary practice for sustaining
the hope without which we cannot continue to function
in our difficult roles. As a leader in social activism told
me, "Sabbath has become for me a practice of loving
the world as it is, even as I long for change. Part of the
change I long for is related to systems I've been in that
don't always have transparency about power. Sabbath
is knowing that that longing is something God has
placed in me but that ultimately God is holding what
I long for." Without being able to rest in that bigger
vision, how would any of us go on? There is a promised

"end" that our lives point to; how good it is to know that we are not it.

Companion for the Journey:
Margaret of Scotland

Only the most determined pilgrims can find it: a tiny building on the edge of a parking lot in Dunfermline just across the Firth of Forth from Edinburgh. But enter the door that then opens to a tunnel, descend eighty-seven stairs, and you will enter St. Margaret's Cave, where almost a thousand years ago, the queen of Scotland found quiet. As the mother of eight children, known for her many acts of charity, it was likely a treasured treat. Legend has it that, once, her husband saw her sneaking out of their home and assumed she must be meeting up with another man. He followed her. No. Hidden in the woods, along a bubbling creek, it was simply her place to "be." Feeling guilty, he decided to decorate the place for her.

The story of Margaret and her husband Malcolm has echoes of the fairytale "Beauty and the Beast." Margaret was a beautiful princess of Magyar and Saxon heritage, born and raised in Hungary, with her teen years spent in the court of King Edward the Confessor in England. After the death of Edward, having lost their sponsor, Margaret's family tried to flee back to Hungary but were blown off course in a storm and forced to seek shelter in a bay now called "St. Margaret's Hope" in Scotland.

Scotland was not England, and the king of Scotland was not like the royalty Margaret had known. Malcolm—nicknamed "Canmore" or "Big Head"— was known to be brutish and warlike. He lived in a fortlike tower, not a palace. He was widowed and already had several sons. During his thirty-five-year reign from 1058 to 1093, he invaded England no fewer than five times, leaving a swath of utter destruction everywhere he went. The English chroniclers of the time have not one kind thing to say about him. But the king was smitten with Margaret and, seemingly, she with him. The two were married in spring 1070. Was this a political marriage? Surely. But all accounts indicate they had genuine affection for one another and that Malcolm denied her little.

Malcolm knew that Margaret would pray in the middle of the night; over time, he came to join her. Malcolm knew she loved to read from the gospels, so he rebound her copy with a gold, bejeweled cover. Malcolm knew she would gather up three hundred hungry persons at a time to feed them, so he helped serve at the table. Malcolm knew she would regularly give away his wealth; he never stopped her. Malcolm knew she wanted to strengthen and unify Christian practice in Scotland, so when she called together the monks and priests for a three-day council to discuss matters, he translated for her.

One of Margaret's dearest causes was that of honoring the Sabbath. In *Life of Margaret*, written by her priest-confessor Turgot, it speaks of Margaret confronting the clergy at the council. "It was another custom of theirs to neglect the reverence due to the Lord's Day by devoting themselves to every kind of worldly business upon it, just as they did upon other days. . . . 'Let us venerate the Lord's Day,' she said, 'because of the resurrection of our Lord which happened upon that day, and let us no longer do servile works upon it.'"[9] Turgot goes on to say that Margaret argued her points so well that "from this time forward these prudent men paid such respect to her earnestness that no one dared on these days either to carry any burdens himself or to compel another to do so."[10] Indeed, since the time of Margaret, Scotland's Christians have been particularly well known for their commitment to Sabbath, so much so that Scottish Sabbath practices, especially on the outer islands, continue to draw journalists from National Geographic[11] and the BBC.[12]

Margaret and Malcolm had six sons and two daughters with each other. Three of these sons eventually became kings of Scotland, including David who ruled from 1124 to 1153 and is still considered one of Scotland's most beloved kings. Their two daughters married Henry I of England and Eustace III of Boulogne, expanding the family's influence.

The one thing that Malcolm never gave to Margaret, however, was peace. While the stories about Margaret emphasize the tremendous influence she had on him and the larger culture of Scotland, the vision of a peaceable kingdom always lay out in the future, never to be realized in her own day. In fall 1093, Malcolm set off with two of their sons, Edward and Edgar, to again raid Northumbria. Malcolm and Edward were killed in battle on November 13. Margaret, who was already ill, died upon hearing the news three days later.

For many years, the couple were buried separately—Malcolm at Tynemouth Priory near Newcastle upon Tyne and Margaret at the Church of the Holy Trinity, which she had built in Dunfermline near her beloved cave. When she was canonized in 1250, however, her remains were to be reinterred in the new Dunfermline Abbey, where Malcolm's remains had also been moved. Legend is that as they moved her casket past his, suddenly it became too heavy to carry and the bearers were forced to set it on the ground. An elder monk is said to have exclaimed, "The queen desires that in death her husband should share her honors as in life she shared his!" Malcolm's body was again disinterred, and the two were buried together. Margaret could not enjoy her final rest without ensuring he enjoyed his final rest as well.

For Reflection

- How does your understanding of the created world change when you think of *menuha* as the "end" of creation rather than the creation of humans?

- What was your notion of "keeping the Sabbath" when you were growing up? How do you tend to think about Sabbath now? In what ways do you try to honor Sabbath?

- Do you agree that the commandment to keep the Sabbath is one of the most dismissed and least understood? Why? Do you have any ideas for rectifying this?

- How do you try to honor others' Sabbath time as a leader? What guardrails have you put in place to help you do so?

- What do you glean from the life of Margaret of Scotland about the spirituality of power, especially as it relates to honoring the Sabbath?

Conclusion

Two thousand years ago today (give or take a decade), a construction worker from Nazareth left his day job to announce the long-promised coming of the reign of God. After years of working with his hands to build shelters, he began to use his words to build a community, ordered toward justice and hospitality. Wherever he went, he gathered people, often at table, to foster new connections among people who might never ordinarily eat with one another.

He broke some boundaries that were no longer serving the common good, even as he fiercely watched out for the needs of the "little ones" of the earth. He asked hard questions—far more than he was willing to answer. He did not hesitate to judge the actions of those who protected only their own interests. He offered cover to those robbed of their dignity. And as the crowds grew, he shared his power with his disciples so they could multiply exponentially what he had created.

Anyone who was not against him, he considered on his side. But there were some who *were* against him—other persons of power who found his work on behalf of God's kingdom threatening to their own interests. He resisted the temptation to sacrifice his deepest dream for his own life. His passion and death

224REDEEMING POWER

224 REDEEMING POWER

on the Cross were the result of his undying passion for the reign of God. And the grave could not hold him bound. In him, the promised seventh day—the fullness of peace and wholeness—already exists.

So just who did he think he was?

The most traditional response to that question has been "God." And it makes sense, doesn't it? Jesus's whole life was about engaging in the same kinds of activities that God engages in throughout scripture, first evidenced in the creation stories of Genesis.

Another ancient response to that question since the time of St. Paul, however, has been "Adam," the New Adam. If all of human history, as Abraham Heschel has claimed, is the story of God in search of man—one who would finally fully live the human vocation on earth and be God's representative within creation— then the gospels are a story of success. As Christians, we readily acknowledge Jesus as true God. Sometimes we might forget that he was also the first *true* man—the first human to exercise dominion in the way that God had imagined from the beginning.

Yet God's search goes on. As the German mystic Meister Eckhart says, "Here in time we make holiday because the eternal birth which God the Father bore and bears unceasingly in eternity is now born in time, in human nature. . . . But if it happens not in me what does it profit me? What matters is that it shall happen in me."[1] What matters is that each of us, in imitation of

Jesus, live fully into *our* human vocation and become *truly* human.

So just who do you think *you* are?

I hope that, if you've read to these concluding pages of the book, you are feeling ever more confident in claiming your identity as a person of power. I hope you feel comfortable naming your power as a positive, even if complicated, reality. I hope you see yourself as God's image, God's representative on earth, even as you are among eight billion others with that same vocation. I hope you experience your power as abundant, even when it seems scarce. I hope you see your power as having a purpose, even when sometimes it feels as if nothing is changing for the better at all.

I hope that your leadership is for you a joy and not just a weight. I hope that you delight in all the things you can do, even as you are aware of the dangers having "power over" can bring. I hope you are conscientious but not anxious, open to learning while not overwhelmed by all the learning yet to be had. I hope that you will never run from your power because you are afraid of it. I hope that all you still can't do will never stand in the way of doing what you can.

I hope that the next time someone looks at you with eyebrow raised and says, "Just who do you think you are?" with full confidence and full humility, you, too, can look them in the eye and respond, "I am Adam."

Acknowledgments

Rav Nahman bar Yitzhak said: Why are Torah matters likened to a tree, as it is stated: "It is a tree of life to them who lay hold upon it" (Proverbs 3:18)? This verse comes to tell you that just as a small piece of wood can ignite a large piece, so too, minor Torah scholars can sharpen great Torah scholars and enable them to advance in their studies. And this is what Rabbi Hanina said: I have learned much from my teachers and even more from my friends, but from my students I have learned more than from all of them.

—Ta'anit 7

I am very grateful to Eileen Ponder of Ave Maria Press who planted the idea for this book in my imagination. While I was off ruminating fruitlessly on the topic of time (a longtime hobby of mine), she nudged, "I think people are asking lots of questions about power right now." I immediately knew what she said was true. The reason I was getting nowhere with writing about time was that I was dealing daily with issues related to power. Eileen has been not only a great editor but also a wonderful thought partner on this project.

I am very grateful to the Collegeville Institute at St. John's University. Without the support of the institute's Killian McDonnell Fellowship in Faith and Culture, I would never have been able to get away for the amount of time needed to jumpstart the writing of this book. And without the beautiful walking paths that wind through and around the campus, I would never have found the inspiration to keep going.

I am very grateful to so many of my leadership colleagues in both the Christian and Jewish worlds who readily said yes to my request for an interview on the topic of power and helped me to understand both Jesus's exercise of power and the Genesis creation stories from a wealth of perspectives. Many of these conversations have been recorded and selections have been worked into the form of podcasts that are now available via my website: anngarrido.com.

In reverse alphabetical order (because the Zs will go first in the kingdom of God), thank you to Bishop Michael Warfel; Anne Marie Vega; Dr. Tim Uhl; Bishop David Toups; Joyce Tibbitts; Joann Terranova; Casey Stanton; David Spotanski; Kerry Robinson; Brett Reinert; Fr. Todd Philipsen; Fr. Jeffrey Ott, OP; Leticia Ochoa Adams; Rhonda Miska; Mary Mirrione; Dr. Elsie Miranda; Sr. Megan McElroy, OP; Or Mars; Dr. Crystal LeRoy; Fr. John Thomas Lane, SSS; Sr. Diane Kennedy, OP; Rev. Jenny Ho Huan; Sheila Heen; Danielle

Harrison; Trinka Hamel; Bishop Gary Gordon; Dennis Gonzalez; Michael Garrido; Rabbi Barry Friedman; Laura Fanucci; Darren Eultgen; Sr. Suzanne Cooke, RSCJ; Dr. Jared Bryson; Lisa Brown; Dr. Elizabeth Unni Berkes; Fr. Michael Bechard; Dr. Kevin Baxter; and Dr. Erin Barisano. Additional tech and editing support for this project was offered by Micah Garrido; Fr. Scott Steinkerchner, OP; Autumn Domingue; and the amazing team at Ave Maria Press.

Finally, I am so very grateful to my "students"—all those whom I've had the chance to teach or facilitate in recent years whether in a classroom, a workshop, or a webinar. It is questions that surfaced from participants in these settings that forced me to realize I needed to take the topic of power far more seriously in my teaching. I am especially grateful to fellows from the Wexner Foundation for Jewish Leadership whose questions were the most difficult of all and continue to help me refine my thinking. *Toda raba*.

Notes

Introduction

1. John Emerich Edward Dalberg-Acton, "Appendix: Letter to Bishop Creighton," in *Historical Essays and Studies*, ed. John Neville Figgis and Reginald Vere Laurence (London: Macmillan, 1907), 504. The actual full quote is: "Power tends to corrupt, and absolute power corrupts absolutely."

2. Max Weber, *Wirtschaft und Gesellschaft: Grundriss der Verstehenden Soziologie*, 5th ed. (Tubingen: Mohr, 1985), 28. Sometimes "possibility" will also be translated "probability."

3. Charles Wright Mills, *The Power Elite*, New ed. (Oxford: Oxford University Press, 2000), 171.

4. Niccolò Machiavelli, "The Prince," The Project Gutenberg, trans. W. K. Marriott, last modified July 1, 2022, https://www.gutenberg.org/files/1232/1232-h/1232-h.htm. The full quote is: "He who makes another powerful ruins himself, for he makes the other so either by shrewdness or force, and both of these qualities are feared by the one who becomes powerful."

5. "Among all the Scriptural texts about creation, the first three chapters of Genesis occupy a unique place. From a literary standpoint, these texts may have had diverse sources. The inspired authors have placed them at the beginning of Scripture to express in their solemn language the truths of creation—its origin and its end in God, its order and goodness, the vocation of man, and finally the drama of sin and the hope of salvation" (*CCC*, 289).

6. In both stories of creation, scripture scholars are in agreement that the word for the first human (*adam*) is a play on the word for the earth (*adamah*) and not a gendered, proper name—that is, Adam. Somewhere in the early chapters of Genesis, however, this shift does take place, and Adam is clearly a proper name by the end of Genesis 4. Scholars are not in agreement about when it is best to consider it such. In this book, I'll tend to start using Adam as a proper name

in any references after Genesis 2:22 when the woman is fashioned from the first human's rib.

7. For an especially helpful chart detailing examples, see the Genesis volume in the Berit Olam: Studies in Hebrew Narrative and Poetry series (Collegeville, MN: Liturgical Press, 2003), 10.

8. I had already been thinking about Genesis as a different starting point for talking about power when I came across Andy Crouch's wonderful book *Playing God: Redeeming the Gift of Power* (Downers Grove, IL: IVP Books, 2013). I am particularly grateful to him for highlighting the "teeming and swarming" dimension of creation and the freedom implied in the phrase "Let it be."

9. Baruch Spinoza is often credited with being the first one to make this connection between *potentia* and *potestas* in his writing, specifically in *Tractatus Politicus* written shortly before his death in 1677.

1. Exercising the Power to Work with Our Hands

1. I appreciate this contrast first pointed out to me in Crouch, *Playing God*, 32–35.

2. Rabbi Shelomo Yitzhaki (1040–1105), quoted in Avivah Gottlieb Zornberg, *Genesis: The Beginning of Desire* (Philadelphia: The Jewish Publication Society, 1995), 18.

3. Maria Montessori, *The Secret of Childhood* (Hyderabad, India: Orient BlackSwan, 2009), 200. More quotes from Montessori on the topic of children and work can be found at https://montessori-ami.org/resource-library/quotes/childs-work.

4. Jana M. Iverson and Susan Goldin-Meadow, "Gesture Paves the Way for Language Development," *Psychological Science* 16, no. 5 (2005): 367–71.

5. Susan Goldin-Meadow, "Using Our Hands to Change Our Minds," *WIREs Cognitive Science* 8, nos. 1–2 (January–April 2017): e1368.

6. Colin McGinn, *Prehension: The Hand and the Emergence of Humanity* (Cambridge, MA: MIT Press, 2015), 39–50.

7. Mike Rose, "The Deepest Meanings of Intelligence and Vocation," interview with Krista Tippet, January 7, 2020, in *On Being*, podcast, last updated October 7, 2021, https://onbeing.org/programs/mike-rose-the-deepest-meanings-of-intelligence-and-vocation.

8. Maria Montessori, quoted in E. M. Standing, *Maria Montessori: Her Life and Work* (New York: Plume, 1998), 21.

9. Pietro Tacchi Venturi, letter to Maria Montessori, September 23, 1817, "Maria Montessori e le sue reti di relazioni," in *Analli di storia dell'educazione e delle istituzioni scolastiche*, no. 25 (Brescia, Italy: Marcelliana, 2018), 31.

10. Elizabeth Warfield, "Montessori's Epiphany with Sherry Mock," January 5, 2021, in *The Good Shepherd and the Child*, podcast, episode 28, https://www.cgsusa.org/episode-28.

11. Giovanna Alatri, *Il mondo al femminile di Maria Montessori: regine, dame, e altre donne* (Roma: Fefè Editore, 2015), 62. Concerning this event, she recorded in her own diary, "On Christmas night 1910—he was born and remained—with us."

12. "About Montessori," National Association for Montessori in the Public Sector, public-montessori.org.

13. Ann Garrido, *Preaching with Children* (Chicago: Liturgy Training Publications, 2022), 11.

14. Elizabeth Warfield, "History of Montessori with Carol Dittberner," October 12, 2021, in *The Good Shepherd and the Child*, podcast, episode 48, https://www.cgsusa.org/episode-48.

2. Exercising the Power to Speak

1. For an exploration of the various associations of naming in Genesis, see Arthur Walker-Jones, "Naming the Human Animal: Genesis 1–3 and Other Animals in Human Becoming," *Zygon* 52, no. 4 (December 2017): 1013–15.

2. For one study related to this observation, see Andrea Taverna et al., "Naming the Living Things: Linguistic, Experiential, and Cultural Factors in Wichí and Spanish Speaking Children," *Journal of Cognition and Culture* 14 (2014): 213–33.

3. For a lovely reflection on this theme, see Romano Guardini's chapter "The Name of God," in *Sacred Signs*, 56–58 (St. Louis, MO: Pio Decimo Press, 1956).

4. For an introduction to the uniqueness of Jesus's parables in contrast to other stories of his time, see part 1 of Gerhard Lohfink, *The Forty Parables of Jesus* (Collegeville, MN: Liturgical Press, 2021). Lohfink notes Jesus used several techniques now regarded as especially effective at capturing the attention of hearers, including using few words to say a great deal, starting in the middle of a plot and stopping before it was resolved, allowing stories to unfold in dialogue rather than prose, and giving access to the internal voice of key characters.

5. See, especially, Mark 8:32, John 7:26, John 11:14, John 16:25, and John 18:20.

6. In one of Euripidis's plays called *The Phoenician Women* from the early fifth century BC, the mother Jocasta converses with her son Polyneices who has been forced to live in exile:

Jocasta:	This above all I long to know: What is an exile's life? Is it a great misery?
Polyneices:	The greatest; worse in reality than in report.
Jocasta:	Worse in what way? What chiefly galls an exile's heart?
Polyneices:	The worst is this: right of free speech does not exist.
Jocasta:	That's a slave's life—to be forbidden to speak one's mind.
Polyneices:	One has to endure the idiocy of those who rule.

Quoted in Michel Foucault, "Discourse and Truth: The Problematization of Parrhesia" (lectures, University of California at Berkeley, October–November 1983), Explore Parrhesia, 9, https:// foucault.info/parrhesia.

7. Dacher Keltner, Deborah H. Gruenfeld, and Cameron Anderson, "Power, Approach, and Inhibition," *Psychological Review* 110, no. 2 (2003): 265–84.

8. For a copy of the letter between David Spotanski and then bishop Wilton Gregory, see Bill McGarvey, "One Parent's Demand for Justice," Busted Halo, May 10, 2010, https://bustedhalo.com/ministry-resources/one-parents-demand-for-justice. For an account of Gregory's also courageous response, see David Spotanski, "As a Church Leader, Cardinal Gregory Has Always 'Put the Rest of Us First,'" *Catholic Standard*, December 2, 2020, https://cathstan.org/voices/david-spotanski/as-a-church-leader-cardinal-gregory-has-always-put-the-rest-of-us-first.

9. Gregory the Great, *The Life of St. Benedict*, XXIII-1, found in Terrence G. Kardong, *The Life of St. Benedict by Gregory the Great, Translation and Commentary* (Collegeville, MN: Liturgical Press, 2009), 91.

10. Raymond DeMallie and Hilda Neihardt, eds., *The Sixth Grandfather: Black Elk's Teachings Given to John G. Neihardt* (Lincoln, NE: Bison Books, 1984), 129.

11. John G. Neihardt, *Black Elk Speaks: The Complete Edition* (Lincoln, NE: University of Nebraska Press, 2014), 262.

12. John Fire/Lame Deer and Richard Erdoes, *Lame Deer, Seeker of Visions* (New York: Simon and Schuster, 1972), 228.

13. Michael F. Steltenkamp, *Nicholas Black Elk* (Norman: University of Oklahoma Press, 2009), 64.

14. Michael F. Steltenkamp, *Black Elk, Holy Man of the Oglala* (Norman: University of Oklahoma Press, 1993), 67–68.

15. Steltenkamp, *Black Elk*, 121.

16. Steltenkamp, *Black Elk*, 65.

17. DeMallie and Neihardt, *Sixth Grandfather*, 129.

3. Exercising the Power to Order

1. Jon Douglas Levenson, *Creation and the Persistence of Evil: The Jewish Drama of Divine Omnipotence* (San Francisco: Harper and Row, 1994), 122.

2. Levenson, *Creation and the Persistence of Evil*, 47.

3. Gregory the Great, *Dialogues II*, section 1-1. Quoted in Kardong, *Life of St. Benedict*, 1.

4. Prologue of the Rule of St. Benedict, quoted in Lavinia Byrne, *The Life and Wisdom of Benedict* (New York: Alba House, 1998), 17.

5. Benedict of Nursia, "*The Rule of Benedict*: Chapter 3: On Calling the Brethren for Counsel," The Order of Saint Benedict, last modified July 1, 2014, https://www.archive.osb.org/rb/text/toc.html#toc.

6. Benedict of Nursia, "*The Rule of Benedict*: Chapter 22: How the Sisters Are to Sleep," The Order of Saint Benedict, last modified July 1, 2014, https://www.archive.osb.org/rb/text/toc.html#toc.

7. Kardong, *Life of St. Benedict*, 127–28.

4. Exercising the Power to Convene

1. Rashi, quoted in Zornberg, *Genesis*, 4–5.

2. Vilna Gaon, quoted in Nosson Scherman and Meir Zlotowitz, eds., *Bereishis/Genesis: A New Translation with a Commentary Anthologized from Talmudic, Midrashic and Rabbinic Sources*, Art Scroll Tanakh Series (New York: Mesorah Publications, 1995), 69.

3. Legatus is an elite association for top-level Catholic business leaders.

4. Mary Nona McGreal, *Samuel Mazzuchelli: American Dominican* (Notre Dame, IN: Ave Maria Press, 2005), 321.

5. Samuel Mazzuchelli, *The Memoirs of Father Samuel Mazzuchelli, OP* (Chicago: The Priory Press, 1967), 52.

6. Different sources offer slightly different numbers in this regard, but one solidly researched resource is the website of the Sinsinawa Dominicans, http://www.sinsinawa.org/mazzuchelli/builder_church.html.

7. Mazzuchelli, *Memoirs*, 58.

8. Joanna Clark, quoted in Mary Nona McGreal, *Samuel Mazzuchelli, American Dominican* (Notre Dame, IN: Ave Maria Press, 2005), 239.

9. Philomena Dunleavy, quoted in McGreal, *Samuel Mazzuchelli*, 276.

5. Exercising the Power to Bless

1. I am grateful to Andy Crouch for pointing this out in chapter 1 of his book *Playing God*.

2. Gerhard Lohfink, *Between Heaven and Earth: New Explorations of Great Biblical Texts*, trans. Linda M. Maloney (Collegeville: Liturgical Press, 2022), 25.

3. Lohfink, *Between Heaven and Earth*, 25.

4. Niccolò Machiavelli, "The Prince," The Project Gutenberg, trans. W. K. Marriott, last modified July 1, 2022, https://www.gutenberg.org/files/1232/1232-h/1232-h.htm.

5. Sean P. Reynolds, *Multiply the Ministry: A Practical Guide for Grassroots Ministry Empowerment* (Winona, MN: St. Mary's Press, 2001).

6. Jean-Baptiste Blain, *The Life of John Baptist de La Salle*, book 1, trans. Richard Arnandez, ed. Luke Salm (Landover, MD: Lasallian Publications, 2000), 80.

7. "Reims, Rue de Marguerite (Hotel des Postes)," In the Footsteps of De La Salle, https://www.dlsfootsteps.org/cities/reims/hotel-des-postes.

8. Blain, *Life of John Baptist de La Salle*, 80.

9. Blain, *Life of John Baptist de La Salle*, 80.

10. Leo Burkhard and Luke Salm, eds., *Encounters: De La Salle at Parmenie* (Christian Brothers Conference, Lasallian Region of North America, 1983), 53.

11. "Lasallian Education: Continuing the Work of Saint John Baptist de La Salle," St. Mary's University of Minnesota, https://www.smumn.edu/about/our-mission/lasallian-education.

6. Exercising the Power to Draw Boundaries

1. Zornberg, *Genesis*, 5.

2. *Bereshis/Genesis*, vol. 1, translation and commentary by Rabbi Meir Zlotowicz (New York: Mesorah Publications, 1977).

3. Mark Zvi Brettler, *How to Read the Bible* (Philadelphia: The Jewish Publication Society, 2005), 45.

4. Ludwig Edelstein, trans., "The Hippocratic Oath," no. 1, in *Supplements to the Bulletin of the History of Medicine* (Baltimore: Johns Hopkins University Press, 1943).

5. The notion of intrinsic versus imposed boundaries is gleaned from Eileen Schmitz, *Staying in Bounds: Straight Talk on Boundaries for Effective Ministry* (St. Louis, MO: Chalice Press, 2010), especially chap. 3, "A Theological Basis for Boundaries," 51–52.

6. Wikipedia, s.v. "Buganda," last modified June 28, 2023, https://en.wikipedia.org/wiki/Buganda (based on information from H. M. Stanley in 1899 and Conrad P. Kottek).

7. Exercising the Power to Remain Firm

1. C. S. Lewis, *Mere Christianity* (New York: HarperOne, 2001), 142.

2. Julie Diamond, "Under the Influence: What Makes Power Corrupt?" in *Power: A User's Guide* (Santa Fe, NM: Belly Song Press, 2016), e-book.

3. Diamond, "Under the Influence."

4. Diamond, "Under the Influence."

5. Diamond, "Motive: What Makes People Corruptible?" in *Power*.

6. For an introduction to this practice, see "Centering Prayer," Contemplative Outreach, https://www.contemplativeoutreach.org.

7. Barat to Eugénie de Gramont, letter 234, May 29, 1831, quoted in Phil Kilroy, *Madeleine Sophie Barat: A Life* (New York: Paulist Press, 2000), 208.

8. Barat to Césaire Mathieu, November 19, 1842, quoted in Kilroy, *Madeleine Sophie Barat*, 369.

9. Joseph Marie Favre to Louise de Limminghe, May 5, 1830–1832 (year uncertain), quoted in Kilroy, *Madeleine Sophie Barat*, 211.

10. Barat to Emma de Bouchaud, Paris, June 18, 1853, in "A Life Lived in Love and Truth," Madeleine Sophie Barat, http://

madeleinesophiebarat.org/a-life-lived-in-love-and-truth-sophie-barat.html.

11. Barat to Anna de Lommessen, Gratz, Paris, April 20, 1859, in "A Life Lived in Love and Truth."

12. Religious of the Sacred Heart (RSCJ), holy card (St. Louis, MO: Society of the Sacred Heart, n.d.).

13. "International Sacred Heart Schools," Sacred Heart Education, https://www.sacredheartusc.education/schools/international-sacred-heart-schools.

14. "Friday Prayer: Espacio," Society of the Sacred Heart, https://rscj.org/spirituality/revealing-gods-love-in-the-midst-of-uncertainty/friday-reflection-espacio-1.

8. Exercising the Power to Ask Questions

1. Abraham Joshua Heschel, *God in Search of Man* (New York: Farrar, Straus and Giroux, 1955), chap. 13, e-book.

2. Ralbag (also known as Gersonides), quoted in *Bereshis/Genesis*, translation and commentary by Rabbi Meir Zlotowicz (New York: Messorah Publications, 1977), 124.

3. Midrash Aggadah, quoted in *Bereshis/Genesis*, 125–26.

4. Martin B. Copenhaver, *Jesus Is the Question* (Nashville: Abingdon Press, 2014), introduction.

5. Copenhaver, *Jesus Is the Question*, introduction.

6. Diamond, "Under the Influence."

7. The idea of the "one thing" questions comes from the book *Thanks for the Feedback* by Douglas Stone and Sheila Heen (New York: Penguin, 2014). See especially chapter 12.

8. Copenhaver, *Jesus Is the Question*, 48.

9. Rainer Maria Rilke, *Letters to a Young Poet* (New York: Random House, 1986), 34.

10. "1987 Special Report: Sister Thea Bowman," interview with Mike Wallace, *60 Minutes*, YouTube, April 4, 2021, https://www.youtube.com/watch?v=g3xuC0XkG48.

11. Charlene Smith and John Feister, *Thea's Song: The Life of Thea Bowman* (Maryknoll, NY: Orbis, 2009), 140.

12. Smith and Feister, *Thea's Song*, 181.

13. Smith and Feister, *Thea's Song*, 215.

14. Smith and Feister, *Thea's Song*, 261.

15. Michael O'Neill McGrath, *This Little Light: Lessons in Living from Sister Thea Bowman* (Maryknoll, NY: Orbis, 2008), 56.

16. "1987 Special Report."

17. Quoted many places, including https://uscatholic.org/articles/202009/sister-thea-bowman-on-dying-with-dignity.

18. Smith and Feister, *Thea's Song*, 237.

19. "Sr. Thea's Address to U.S. Bishops," YouTube, June 17, 1989, https://www.youtube.com/watch?v=uOV0nQkjuoA.

20. Smith and Feister, *Thea's Song*, 281.

9. Exercising the Power to Judge

1. David A. Hubbard and Glenn W. Barker, *Genesis 1–15*, vol. 1 of *Word Biblical Commentary*, ed. David A. Hubbard and Glenn W. Barker (Waco, TX: Word Books, 1987).

2. David L. Lieber, ed., *Etz Hayim Torah and Commentary* (New York: The Jewish Publication Society, 2001), 13.

3. Eileen Schmitz, *Staying in Bounds: Straight Talk on Boundaries for Effective Ministry* (St Louis, MO: Chalice Press, 2010), 49.

4. "The Historic Sermon of Antonio de Montesinos" as recorded by Bartolome de las Casas and quoted in *Three Dominican Pioneers in the New World: Antonio de Montesinos, Domingo de Betanzos, Gonzalo Lucero*, translation and introduction by Felix Jay (Lewiston, NY: Edwin Mellen Press, 2002), 18.

5. Jay, *Three Dominican Pioneers*, 18.

6. Jay, *Three Dominican Pioneers*, 19.

7. Las Casas, quoted in Jay, *Three Dominican Pioneers*, 26.

8. Mary Nona McGreal, "Preachers from Abroad: 1786–1815," in *Dominicans at Home in a Young Nation: 1786–1865*, vol. 1 of *The Order of Preachers in the United States: A Family History*, ed. Mary Nona McGreal (Strasbourg, France: Editions du Signe, 2001),

https://www.dom.edu/sites/default/files/pdfs/about/McGreal/McGreal_Vol_1_Chap1_Prelude.pdf.

9. McGreal, "Preachers from Abroad." Other sources argue for 1545 but concur that he was martyred for his work on behalf of native peoples.

10. Exercising the Power to Clothe

1. Radak, "Radak on Genesis 3:8," Sefaria, https://www.sefaria.org/Radak_on_Genesis.3.8.2?lang=bi&with=all&lang2=en.

2. "Tractate Derekh Eretz Zutta," chap. 10, Sefaria, https://www.sefaria.org/Tractate_Derekh_Eretz_Zuta.1.1.

3. Gildas Hamel, *Poverty and Charity in Roman Palestine* (Berkeley: University of California Press, 1990), 93–108.

4. Thomas J. Lane, "Jesus as High Priest: The Significance of the Seamless Robe," St. Paul Center for Biblical Theology, July 19, 2019, https://stpaulcenter.com/jesus-as-high-priest-the-significance-of-the-seamless-robe.

5. Augustine of Hippo, *Confessions* 10.54; Thomas Aquinas, *Summa Theologiae* 2–2.167, A.2.

6. Aquinas, *Summa Theologiae* 2–2.112.1; see also 2–2.109.3.1.

7. While the length of the chapter does not permit going into detail about the ethics of confidentiality, for a deeper dive, see Richard Gula, *Ethics in Pastoral Ministry* (New York: Paulist Press, 1996), 117–41, for his excellent chapter on confidentiality in ministry.

8. US Conference of Catholic Bishops, *Procedures for Resolving Conflict* (Washington, DC: Author, 2002), 26. See also *CCC*, 2489: "Charity and respect for the truth should dictate the response to every request for information or communication," the *Catechism of the Catholic Church* notes. "The good and safety of others, respect for privacy, and the common good are sufficient reasons for being silent about what ought not to be known or for making use of discreet language. The duty to avoid scandal often commands strict discretion. No one is bound to reveal the truth to someone who does not have the right to know it."

9. Hildegard of Bingen, *Scivias*, Classics of Western Spirituality (New York: Paulist Press, 1990), 59.

10. Hildegard of Bingen, *The Book of Life's Merits*, 4.38 quoted in Barbara Newman, *Sister of Wisdom* (Berkeley: University of California Press, 1997), 61.

11. Hildegard of Bingen, *The Letters of Hildegard of Bingen*, vol. 3, trans. Joseph L. Baird and Radd K. Ehrman (Oxford: Oxford University Press, 2004), 113.

12. Hildegard of Bingen, *The Book of Divine Works*, 1.4.72, quoted in Sabina Flanagan, ed., *Secrets of God: Writings of Hildegard of Bingen* (Boston: Shambhala, 1996), 69.

11. Exercising the Power to Start Anew

1. Samson Raphael Hirsch, "Rav Hirsch on Torah, Genesis 3:24:1," in *Der Pentateuch. Übersetzt und erläutert von Samson Raphael Hirsch, 1903 [de]*, Sefaria, https://www.sefaria.org/Rav_Hirsch_on_Torah%2C_Genesis.3.24.1.

2. Marianne Williamson, *A Return to Love* (New York: HarperCollins, 1992), 165.

3. Diamond, "Love Your Low Rank," in *Power*.

4. Diamond, "Cultivate Role Conflict," in *Power*.

5. Diamond, "Cultivate Role Conflict," in *Power*.

6. Alfred W. McCoy, "Opium History, 1858–1940," http://www.a1b2c3.com/drugs/opi0101.htm.

7. Sarah Young, letter to her family, recorded in John Gittings, "Lost Souls," *The Guardian*, August 5, 2000, https://www.theguardian.com/world/2000/aug/05/china.johngittings.

12. On Laying Down One's Power

1. Abraham Heschel, *The Sabbath* (New York: Farrar, Straus, and Giroux, 1951), 22–23.

2. Levenson, *Creation and the Persistence of Evil*, 123. "The reality that the Sabbath represents—God's unchallenged and uncompromised mastery, blessing, and hallowing—is consistently

and irreversibly available only in the world-to-come. Until then, it is only known in the tantalizing experience of the Sabbath."

3. Heschel, *Sabbath*, 3.

4. Heschel, *Sabbath*, 6.

5. Heschel, *Sabbath*, 13

6. Quoted in Heschel, *Sabbath*, 17.

7. "Verum autem sabbatum ipsum redemptorem nostrum Iesum Christum Dominum habemus": Epist. 13, 1: CCL 140A, 992.

8. John Paul II, *Dies Domini*, 23. See, especially, this passage: "St. Augustine notes in turn: '. . . In the weekly cycle, however, it is the eighth day after the seventh, that is after the Sabbath, and the first day of the week.' The distinction of Sunday from the Jewish Sabbath grew ever stronger in the mind of the Church, even though there have been times in history when, because the obligation of Sunday rest was so emphasized, the Lord's Day tended to become more like the Sabbath. Moreover, there have always been groups within Christianity which observe both the Sabbath and Sunday as 'two brother days.'

9. Turgot, *Life of Saint Margaret, Queen of Scotland* (Edinburgh, Scotland: W. Paterson, 1884), 49, https://archive.org/details/lifeofstmargaret00turguoft/page/50/mode/2up.

10. Turgot, *Life of Saint Margaret*, 51.

11. Andrew Evans, "Sabbath on Skye," *National Geographic*, September 20, 2013, https://www.nationalgeographic.com/travel/article/sabbath-on-skye.

12. Steven Brocklehurst, "Does the Sabbath Still Exist on the Isle of Lewis?" BBC News, October 24, 2014, https://www.bbc.com/news/uk-scotland-29708202.

Conclusion

1. Meister Eckhart, "This Is Meister Eckhart from Whom God Nothing Hid," sermon, in Franz Pfeiffer, *Meister Eckhart*, trans. C. De B. Evans (London: John M. Watkins, 1924), http://www.faculty.umb.edu/gary_zabel/Courses/Spinoza/Texts/EckSermI.htm.

Ann M. Garrido is associate professor of homiletics at Aquinas Institute of Theology in St. Louis, Missouri, where she previously directed the school's Doctorate of Ministry in Preaching program. Garrido has served as the Marten Faculty Fellow in Homiletics at the University of Notre Dame. She is the author of multiple books, including the award-winning *Redeeming Administration*, *Redeeming Conflict*, and *Let's Talk About Truth*. She travels nationally and internationally helping communities discuss the topics they find toughest to talk about—conversations that often involve questions of power.

anngarrido.com
Facebook: anngarridodmin

MORE BOOKS BY
ANN M. GARRIDO

Redeeming Administration
12 Spiritual Habits for Catholic Leaders
in Parishes, Schools, Religious Communities,
and Other Institutions

Redeeming Conflict
12 Habits for Christian Leaders

Let's Talk about Truth
A Guide for Preachers, Teachers,
and Other Catholic Leaders in a World
of Doubt and Discord

#Rules_of_Engagement
8 Christian Habits for Being Good
and Doing Good Online